FALUN GONG FOR BEGINNERS
AN INTRODUCTION TO ENERGY, MOVEMENT, AND PHILOSOPHY

JEANNIE LEE

The entire cultivation process for a practitioner is one of constantly giving up human attachment.

— LI HONGZHI

CONTENTS

Introduction to Falun Gong: Unveiling a Spiritual Movement — xi

1. THE HISTORICAL ROOTS OF FALUN GONG — 1
   - The Evolution of Qigong in Chinese Culture — 1
   - Daoist and Buddhist Influences — 3
   - The Role of Qi in Traditional Practices — 4
   - How Falun Gong Differentiates Itself — 5
   - Early Practitioners and Their Contributions — 6
   - Government Support and Early Recognition — 8
   - Growth During the Qigong Boom — 9

2. LI HONGZHI AND THE ESTABLISHMENT OF FALUN GONG — 11
   - Early Life and Inspirations of Li Hongzhi — 11
   - Founding of Falun Gong in 1992 — 12
   - Key Teachings of the Master — 14
   - Public Lectures and Global Outreach — 15
   - The Philosophy Behind the Practice — 16
   - The Debate Around His Persona — 18
   - Legacy and Leadership — 19

3. THE CORE PRINCIPLES OF FALUN GONG — 21
   - Truthfulness (Zhen) — 21
   - Compassion (Shan) — 22
   - Forbearance (Ren) — 24
   - Integration with Personal Morality — 25
   - The Role of Karma in Daily Life — 26
   - Spiritual Ascension Through Practice — 27
   - Balancing Material and Spiritual Goals — 29

4. THE PRACTICE OF FALUN GONG — 31
   - Introduction to the Five Exercises — 31
   - The Meditative Focus of Falun Gong — 32
   - Physical and Spiritual Benefits — 34

Creating a Daily Practice Routine	35
The Role of Group Practice	36
Challenges in Developing Consistency	37
The Impact of Practice on Health	39

5. **ZHUAN FALUN: THE CENTRAL TEXT** — 41
   - Structure and Organization of *Zhuan Falun* — 41
   - Key Concepts Explained — 42
   - The Universe, Time, and Space in Falun Gong — 44
   - Understanding the Law Wheel (Falun) — 45
   - Practical Teachings for Self-Improvement — 46
   - Common Misinterpretations of *Zhuan Falun* — 48
   - Its Impact on Falun Gong Practitioners — 49

6. **THE ROLE OF FALUN GONG IN MODERN SPIRITUALITY** — 51
   - Bridging Eastern and Western Beliefs — 51
   - Connection to Global Movements — 52
   - Adapting Traditional Practices for Modern Times — 54
   - How Practitioners Incorporate Falun Gong Daily — 55
   - Resonance with Universal Spiritual Truths — 56
   - Public Perceptions in a Global Context — 58
   - Maintaining Purity of the Practice — 59

7. **THE CHINESE GOVERNMENT'S RESPONSE** — 62
   - Initial Support and Promotion — 62
   - The 1999 Crackdown — 63
   - Key Events in the Suppression Campaign — 65
   - Media Portrayal of Falun Gong — 66
   - Legal and Social Ramifications for Practitioners — 68
   - Resistance and Advocacy by Practitioners — 69
   - Ongoing International Implications — 70

8. **THE FALUN GONG DIASPORA** — 73
   - Growth of Falun Gong Communities Abroad — 73
   - The Role of Western Advocacy — 75
   - Building International Awareness — 76
   - The Establishment of Media Platforms — 78

    Bridging Cultural Gaps in Practice   79
    Collaboration with Global Human Rights
    Groups   81
    The Future of Falun Gong Outside China   82

9. CONTROVERSIES AND CRITICISMS   85
    Allegations Against the Practice   85
    Challenges of Verifying Claims   86
    Separating Fact from Fiction   88
    Internal Conflicts Among Practitioners   89
    Addressing Skepticism and Opposition   91
    How Practitioners Respond to Criticisms   92
    The Role of Objectivity in Understanding
    Falun Gong   94

10. THE HEALTH BENEFITS OF FALUN GONG   96
    Scientific Studies on Meditation and Health   96
    Testimonials from Practitioners   98
    The Role of Mind-Body Connection   99
    Strengthening Mental Resilience   100
    Addressing Chronic Illnesses Through Practice   102
    Challenges in Establishing Evidence   103
    Falun Gong as a Complementary Practice   104

11. FALUN GONG IN POPULAR CULTURE   107
    Depictions in Media and Literature   107
    Artistic Expressions Inspired by Falun Gong   108
    Documentaries and Advocacy Films   110
    Role of Shen Yun in Cultural Outreach   111
    Public Figures and Falun Gong   113
    Cultural Contributions by Practitioners   114
    Evolving Image of Falun Gong   116

12. THE PATH FORWARD FOR FALUN GONG   118
    Adapting to a Changing World   118
    Challenges Facing Future Generations   119
    Strengthening Practitioner Communities   121
    Addressing Modern Skepticism   123
    Continued Advocacy for Human Rights   124
    Embracing Technology and Modern Outreach   125
    The Vision for Falun Gong's Future   127

Conclusion 129
Glossary 139
Suggested Readings 145

INTRODUCTION TO FALUN GONG: UNVEILING A SPIRITUAL MOVEMENT

ORIGINS AND FOUNDATIONS OF FALUN GONG

Falun Gong emerged in the early 1990s in China, a period when qigong practices were flourishing. Rooted in traditional Chinese culture, it presented itself as a blend of physical exercises and spiritual teachings aimed at improving health and character. Unlike other forms of qigong, Falun Gong claimed to be more than just a health regimen; it was a path to enlightenment. The practice's emphasis on truthfulness, compassion, and forbearance quickly distinguished it from the growing field of wellness practices in China.

Falun Gong's founder positioned the practice as a return to ancient wisdom. Drawing on Confucian, Daoist, and Buddhist principles, it aimed to reconnect practitioners with a sense of cosmic order. By aligning their behaviors and thoughts with universal principles, followers believed they could achieve both physical vitality and spiritual transcendence. This dual promise of health and enlightenment attracted millions, spanning diverse demographics across China.

As the movement gained traction, its simplicity stood out. There were no formal memberships, no fees, and no rigid institutional structures. Practitioners gathered in parks and public spaces, performing slow, deliberate movements while discussing philosophical teachings. This accessibility fostered a grassroots explosion of interest, making Falun Gong one of the most popular spiritual practices in modern Chinese history.

Yet, its rise wasn't without challenges. The Chinese government, initially supportive of qigong practices for their health benefits, began to view Falun Gong with suspicion as its growing popularity hinted at organizational potential. These early tensions would later escalate into a dramatic and contentious chapter in the movement's history.

THE ROLE OF LI HONGZHI

Li Hongzhi, the founder of Falun Gong, played a pivotal role in shaping its identity. Born in 1951 in Gongzhuling, China, Li's life story has been a point of fascination and debate. He presented himself not just as a teacher but as someone with profound spiritual insights, a figure capable of bridging ancient wisdom and modern society. His teachings were delivered in a charismatic and authoritative style, capturing the imaginations of his followers.

Li's core message revolved around moral integrity and self-cultivation. He emphasized that personal growth required aligning with the principles of truthfulness, compassion, and forbearance. Through anecdotes, metaphors, and sometimes enigmatic statements, Li wove a narrative that painted Falun Gong as a practice rooted in universal truths. His ability to communicate complex ideas in an accessible manner earned him both admiration and scrutiny.

The founder's public persona added to the intrigue. He claimed to possess extraordinary abilities, including the power to heal and the capacity to perceive higher dimensions. For believers, these claims reinforced their faith in the practice. For skeptics, they fueled criticism and suspicion. Li's statements about science, the cosmos, and human existence sparked debates, drawing both fervent supporters and vocal detractors.

As the leader of the movement, Li maintained a strategic distance from formal hierarchies. This lack of centralized control allowed Falun Gong to spread organically but also left room for misinterpretations of his teachings. His decision to move to the United States in the late 1990s added another layer of complexity, as it coincided with the Chinese government's escalating crackdown on the practice.

SPIRITUAL PRACTICES AND PHILOSOPHIES

Falun Gong's spiritual framework is built on the principles of truthfulness, compassion, and forbearance, which are considered the cornerstones of personal and societal harmony. These principles are not just abstract ideals but practical guidelines for daily living. Practitioners are encouraged to reflect on their actions, cultivate kindness, and endure hardships with grace, believing that such virtues lead to a purified mind and body.

Central to the philosophy is the concept of karma and virtue. Karma, seen as the accumulation of bad deeds, is believed to cause suffering and misfortune. Virtue, on the other hand, is earned through good deeds and selflessness. By aligning their actions with higher moral standards, practitioners aim to reduce their karma and increase their virtue, setting the stage for spiritual elevation.

The practice also emphasizes introspection and self-awareness. Followers are taught to identify and relinquish attachments, whether to material possessions, personal desires, or negative emotions. This process is seen as essential for achieving spiritual clarity and aligning with the cosmic order. The idea of "cultivation" goes beyond the physical, extending into the moral and spiritual domains of life.

Falun Gong's teachings often draw on metaphysical concepts, such as the existence of higher dimensions and the interplay between the physical and spiritual worlds. These ideas are presented as both profound truths and practical guidance, creating a worldview that merges traditional Chinese philosophy with modern existential concerns.

While the philosophies are deeply spiritual, they are also framed as accessible and universal. This duality allows Falun Gong to resonate with a broad audience, from those seeking inner peace to those exploring deeper existential questions.

RELATIONSHIP WITH TRADITIONAL QIGONG

At first glance, Falun Gong appears to share much in common with traditional qigong practices. Both involve physical exercises, meditative techniques, and a focus on energy flow within the body. However, Falun Gong sets itself apart by embedding its exercises within a rich spiritual context. Unlike qigong, which is often secular, Falun Gong presents itself as a complete system of moral and spiritual cultivation.

The practice's relationship with qigong is both a strength and a source of contention. On one hand, its physical exercises are straightforward and align with established qigong traditions, making them accessible to beginners. On the other hand, its emphasis on moral and spiritual growth elevates it to a philosophical system, challenging the boundaries of what qigong is traditionally understood to be.

Falun Gong's divergence from traditional qigong can also be seen in its approach to health and healing. While most qigong practices focus on balancing the body's energy to improve physical well-being, Falun Gong teaches that true health comes from moral rectitude and spiritual alignment. Physical exercises are secondary to the cultivation of the mind and heart, a perspective that redefines the purpose of practice.

The movement's reinterpretation of qigong has led to mixed reactions. Some view it as an innovative fusion of ancient and modern ideas, while others see it as a departure from traditional practices. This duality has fueled both its appeal and its controversies, placing Falun Gong at the crossroads of tradition and innovation.

CORE TEXTS: ZHUAN FALUN AND OTHER TEACHINGS

At the heart of Falun Gong's teachings lies *Zhuan Falun*, a book authored by Li Hongzhi. This text serves as the movement's foundational scripture, outlining its principles, philosophies, and practices. Written in a conversational yet authoritative tone, *Zhuan Falun* explores profound topics, from the nature of the universe to the intricacies of human behavior.

The book is structured around a series of lectures, each delving into different aspects of the practice. It combines metaphysical concepts with practical advice, creating a guide that is both spiritual and pragmatic. *Zhuan Falun* is often seen as a living text, one that reveals new insights with each reading, reflecting the evolving understanding of its readers.

In addition to *Zhuan Falun*, Li Hongzhi has authored other texts and delivered numerous lectures that expand on the practice's core teachings. These works provide a comprehensive framework for understanding Falun Gong, addressing questions ranging from the philosophical to the practical. Together, they form a cohesive body of knowledge that guides practitioners on their spiritual journey.

The core texts are not merely instructional but inspirational. They challenge readers to think critically, question assumptions, and strive for personal growth. This intellectual and spiritual engagement is one of the reasons why Falun Gong has resonated with such a diverse audience, transcending cultural and geographical boundaries.

Through its writings, Falun Gong positions itself as a path to self-discovery and universal truth. Its texts invite readers to explore not just the practice but their place in the cosmos, creating a narrative that is both deeply personal and profoundly universal.

MEDITATION AND EXERCISE ROUTINES

The physical aspect of Falun Gong revolves around five meditative exercises, which are simple yet meticulously designed to align the body's energy with its spiritual practices. These exercises are practiced in a calm, rhythmic manner, often accompanied by soothing music or verbal instructions. Each movement is deliberate and purposeful, aimed at fostering physical relaxation and mental clarity. Unlike intense workout regimens, the exercises are accessible to people of all ages and fitness levels, emphasizing harmony instead of exertion.

The first four exercises involve standing movements, which vary from gentle stretching to motions meant to facilitate energy flow. These exercises are said to open up energy channels in the body, releasing blockages that may cause physical or mental discomfort. Practitioners often describe the process as invigorating yet calming, akin to a recharge of the mind and body. The movements are methodical, offering a meditative rhythm that encourages practitioners to focus inwardly.

The fifth exercise is a seated meditation that requires stillness and deep concentration. Practitioners cross their legs in the lotus or half-lotus position, close their eyes, and maintain a serene demeanor. This exercise is designed to cultivate inner peace and a connection to higher realms of existence. Unlike other meditation practices that focus purely on mindfulness, Falun Gong's seated meditation integrates its spiritual principles, aiming for a transformative experience that transcends the mundane.

These exercises are not only physical but also deeply symbolic. They are said to mirror the principles of truthfulness, compassion, and forbearance, manifesting these values in a tangible form. Each motion or posture is imbued with meaning, creating a bridge between the physical and the metaphysical. Practitioners often remark that the exercises become a spiritual journey, offering insights into both their inner selves and the world around them.

The routines are typically practiced in group settings, fostering a sense of community and shared purpose. Parks, open spaces, and even private homes become places of quiet introspection and collective energy. This communal aspect of the exercises reinforces the practice's emphasis on interconnectedness, reminding participants that their journey is both individual and collective.

MISCONCEPTIONS AND PUBLIC PERCEPTIONS

Falun Gong has faced an array of misconceptions and polarized opinions since its inception. To some, it is a peaceful spiritual practice that offers profound personal benefits. To others, it is a source of controversy and misunderstanding. Much of the confusion stems from the practice's rapid rise in popularity, coupled with its clash with political and cultural norms, particularly in China.

One common misconception is that Falun Gong is a religion. While it shares similarities with religious practices—such as moral teachings and meditative exercises—it lacks formal structures like clergy, temples, or rituals. Practitioners often describe it as a cultivation practice, emphasizing personal growth and alignment with universal principles rather than worship or doctrine. This distinction is crucial yet often overlooked, leading to mislabeling by media and critics.

Another point of contention is the portrayal of Falun Gong as a secretive or fringe group. The movement's decentralized nature, combined with its esoteric teachings, has sometimes been misinterpreted as exclusivity. However, practitioners emphasize that Falun Gong is open to all and requires no formal membership. The lack of institutional oversight is not secrecy but a reflection of its grassroots origins and emphasis on individual responsibility.

Political narratives, particularly in China, have also shaped public perceptions. The Chinese government's crackdown on Falun Gong in the late 1990s cast the practice in a contentious light, branding it a threat to social stability. State-sponsored propaganda campaigns further muddied the waters, portraying Falun Gong as subversive and dangerous. Outside of China, these narratives often clash with testimonials from practitioners who describe the practice as peaceful and transformative.

Misunderstandings also arise from the metaphysical aspects of Falun Gong's teachings. Concepts such as karma, virtue, and higher dimensions can be challenging to grasp or accept, especially in cultures unfamiliar with such ideas. Critics may dismiss these elements as pseudoscience, while adherents view them as profound truths. This tension underscores the broader challenge of bridging cultural and philosophical divides.

Despite these misconceptions, Falun Gong continues to attract followers worldwide. Its emphasis on truthfulness, compassion, and forbearance resonates across cultural and geographical boundaries. The practice's ability to inspire personal transformation and foster a sense of purpose has created a community that stands resilient in the face of misunderstanding and opposition.

THE HISTORICAL ROOTS OF FALUN GONG

THE EVOLUTION OF QIGONG IN CHINESE CULTURE

Qigong, a term that literally translates to "energy work," has a history that stretches back thousands of years in Chinese culture. It is a practice rooted in the belief that the human body contains an energy force, or *qi*, that can be harnessed and directed for health and vitality. Ancient Chinese texts often describe qigong as a method of cultivating both physical strength and spiritual awareness. From the earliest dynasties to the present, qigong has remained a staple in China's approach to health and wellness.

Originally, qigong was practiced primarily within monastic and elite circles. Monks in remote temples and scholars seeking longevity experimented with breathing techniques and movements that aimed to align the body with the rhythms of nature. These early practitioners believed that controlling the flow of *qi* could unlock both mental clarity and physical resilience. Over time, these techniques filtered down to the general populace, transforming into folk practices passed through generations.

During the 20th century, qigong underwent significant modernization. With advancements in science and a growing interest in traditional health practices, the Chinese government began to promote qigong as a national fitness program. This ushered in a period of revival, where ancient practices were standardized and made accessible to the masses. Qigong became a household term, with millions attending public classes and seminars.

The late 20th century saw an explosion in qigong's popularity, with countless variations springing up across China. Teachers began emphasizing not just physical health but also spiritual growth, merging traditional exercises with philosophical teachings. This period of diversification laid the groundwork for movements like Falun Gong, which adapted qigong principles into something uniquely transformative.

Despite its mainstream appeal, qigong's widespread adoption was not without controversy. Critics questioned the legitimacy of certain practices and expressed concerns about the commercialization of what was once a sacred tradition. These debates set the stage for Falun Gong's emergence, as it sought to reclaim qigong's spiritual and moral dimensions while distinguishing itself from the growing sea of modern adaptations.

DAOIST AND BUDDHIST INFLUENCES

Falun Gong's philosophical foundation owes much to Daoist and Buddhist teachings. Daoism, with its emphasis on harmony with the natural order, provides the backdrop for many of Falun Gong's concepts about energy flow and balance. Meanwhile, Buddhism's focus on self-cultivation and enlightenment informs the practice's moral and spiritual framework. Together, these influences create a rich tapestry of ideas that resonate deeply with practitioners.

From Daoism, Falun Gong borrows the concept of qi and its role in maintaining physical and spiritual harmony. Daoist teachings often describe the universe as a vast, interconnected system where energy flows freely, influencing everything from the growth of plants to the health of individuals. Falun Gong's exercises reflect this understanding, aiming to align the body's energy with the larger cosmic flow.

Buddhist principles manifest in Falun Gong's emphasis on truthfulness, compassion, and forbearance. These virtues mirror the Buddhist path to enlightenment, where one strives to transcend suffering through moral discipline and mindfulness. Falun Gong incorporates these ideals into daily practice, encouraging followers to examine their thoughts and actions critically as a means of spiritual growth.

The synthesis of these traditions is not merely theoretical but practical. Practitioners are encouraged to reflect on their own behaviors, seeking to eliminate attachments and cultivate virtues. This dual focus on inner transformation and outward action mirrors both Daoist and Buddhist approaches to self-improvement, making Falun Gong a deeply holistic practice.

These influences also extend to Falun Gong's cosmology. References to karma, reincarnation, and the interplay between spiritual dimensions draw directly from Buddhist texts, while the concept of universal energy aligns with Daoist metaphysics. This blending of traditions creates a spiritual framework that feels both ancient and innovative, bridging cultural divides while staying rooted in Chinese heritage.

THE ROLE OF QI IN TRADITIONAL PRACTICES

The concept of *qi* is central to traditional Chinese practices, acting as both a philosophical and practical foundation. Often described as the life force or vital energy, *qi* is believed to flow through the body's meridians, influencing physical health and emotional well-being. In traditional medicine, the balance and movement of *qi* are thought to be crucial for preventing illness and maintaining vitality.

In ancient China, the study of *qi* was closely linked to Daoist alchemy and martial arts. Daoist monks developed intricate breathing exercises and meditative techniques designed to enhance the flow of *qi* within the body. These methods were not only meant for health but also for spiritual enlightenment, as the cultivation of *qi* was seen as a path to immortality. Martial artists, meanwhile, used *qi* to improve physical strength, endurance, and agility, embedding the concept deeply into Chinese culture.

Traditional Chinese medicine (TCM) takes a systematic approach to *qi*. Techniques like acupuncture and herbal remedies aim to regulate the flow of *qi*, addressing blockages that are believed to cause physical or emotional imbalances. This medical perspective on *qi* laid the groundwork for practices like qigong and, later, Falun Gong, which use movement and meditation to optimize energy flow.

Falun Gong's exercises are designed with *qi* in mind, though they elevate the concept to a spiritual plane. Unlike other qigong practices that focus on physical health, Falun Gong teaches that *qi* is a reflection of moral and spiritual alignment. Practitioners believe that cultivating virtues like truthfulness and compassion can enhance their *qi*, leading to both physical vitality and spiritual awakening.

The role of *qi* in Falun Gong serves as a bridge between traditional and modern perspectives. It resonates with those familiar with TCM and Daoist practices while offering a broader, more inclusive interpretation. By framing *qi* as both an energy force and a moral compass, Falun Gong transforms an ancient concept into a cornerstone of its unique philosophy.

HOW FALUN GONG DIFFERENTIATES ITSELF

Falun Gong stands out in a sea of qigong practices through its distinct combination of physical exercises, spiritual teachings, and moral principles. While many qigong systems focus solely on health or relaxation, Falun Gong positions itself as a path to personal and cosmic harmony. This dual focus on physical and spiritual cultivation sets it apart from more secular or fragmented approaches.

One key difference is the emphasis on moral character. Falun Gong teaches that personal health and spiritual growth are intrinsically linked to virtues like truthfulness, compassion, and forbearance. This moral framework is not an optional add-on but a core part of the practice, influencing everything from meditation routines to interpersonal interactions. This integration of ethics and exercise is rare among qigong systems, making Falun Gong uniquely holistic.

Another distinguishing feature is its accessibility. Unlike many spiritual practices that require formal memberships, initiation rituals, or fees, Falun Gong is free and open to all. Practitioners can learn its exercises and teachings through books, videos, or public gatherings, removing barriers to entry. This simplicity and inclusivity have helped the practice gain widespread appeal, attracting followers from diverse backgrounds.

Falun Gong also differentiates itself through its texts, particularly *Zhuan Falun*. While most qigong practices rely on oral transmission or fragmented writings, Falun Gong provides a comprehensive guide to its philosophy and methods. This textual foundation allows practitioners to engage deeply with the practice, fostering both intellectual and spiritual exploration.

The practice's relationship with the Chinese government further sets it apart. While most qigong systems enjoy state support or indifference, Falun Gong's rapid growth and philosophical claims drew scrutiny and eventual suppression. This unique historical trajectory has made Falun Gong a symbol of spiritual resilience, shaping its identity on both a personal and global scale.

EARLY PRACTITIONERS AND THEIR CONTRIBUTIONS

The early practitioners of Falun Gong played a vital role in its development and dissemination. These individuals came from diverse backgrounds, ranging from academics and medical professionals to farmers and retirees. What united them was a shared belief in the practice's potential to transform lives, both individually and collectively.

Practitioners often took on the role of teachers, introducing Falun Gong to their communities through informal gatherings in parks or cultural centers. These grassroots efforts created a ripple effect as more people joined and began spreading the practice in their own networks. The lack of formal hierarchies allowed this organic growth, turning Falun Gong into a nationwide phenomenon within a few short years.

Beyond teaching, early practitioners contributed to the practice's visibility through public demonstrations and health fairs. They showcased the exercises and shared testimonials about the benefits they experienced, from improved health to greater emotional resilience. These personal stories resonated with audiences, building trust and curiosity around the practice.

Many early practitioners also documented their experiences, contributing to the growing body of Falun Gong literature. Their writings and reflections provided valuable insights into the practice, serving as both inspiration and instruction for newcomers. These accounts enriched the movement, adding layers of depth and authenticity to its teachings.

Their efforts laid the foundation for Falun Gong's global reach. As the practice spread beyond China, early practitioners continued to serve as ambassadors, introducing its principles to new audiences. Their dedication and adaptability ensured that Falun Gong could thrive in diverse cultural contexts, making it a truly international phenomenon.

GOVERNMENT SUPPORT AND EARLY RECOGNITION

In its infancy, Falun Gong enjoyed a level of government support that might seem surprising given its later controversies. During the late 1980s and early 1990s, the Chinese government actively promoted qigong practices as a means of improving public health and reducing healthcare costs. Within this favorable climate, Falun Gong emerged as a respected and widely practiced form of qigong, earning accolades from various government agencies.

Government recognition came in the form of health awards and endorsements from state-run organizations. Early studies conducted by hospitals and scientific institutions reported improvements in physical health among practitioners. These findings aligned with the government's goals of fostering wellness through traditional practices, giving Falun Gong a stamp of legitimacy in its early years. Practitioners often cited these endorsements as evidence of the practice's effectiveness.

Falun Gong also participated in state-sponsored events, further cementing its relationship with government authorities. Demonstrations at health fairs and public gatherings highlighted the physical and mental benefits of the practice. These events drew large crowds, increasing public awareness and solidifying Falun Gong's reputation as a leading qigong practice. The early 1990s saw the practice flourish under this symbiotic relationship.

However, government support was not without strings. State authorities encouraged qigong organizations to register and conform to official guidelines, ensuring they aligned with national priorities. While Falun Gong initially operated within these parameters, its growing popularity and spiritual claims began to attract scrutiny. The very attention that elevated Falun Gong in its early years would later contribute to its contentious relationship with the state.

This initial period of recognition was instrumental in shaping Falun Gong's rapid growth. It provided a platform for the practice to reach millions of people, fostering a sense of legitimacy and trust. Yet, the dynamics of this relationship also hinted at the tensions to come as the practice's expanding influence began to challenge the boundaries of government tolerance.

GROWTH DURING THE QIGONG BOOM

Falun Gong's rise coincided with what is often referred to as the "Qigong Boom" in China, a period during the 1980s and 1990s when qigong practices surged in popularity. This cultural phenomenon was fueled by a renewed interest in traditional Chinese health practices, combined with a growing openness to alternative approaches to wellness. Millions of people embraced qigong as a way to improve their physical and mental health, creating fertile ground for new movements like Falun Gong.

The Qigong Boom was characterized by diversity and innovation. Teachers from various backgrounds developed unique styles and systems, blending traditional techniques with modern ideas. Public parks and community centers became hubs of activity, as practitioners gathered to perform exercises and share knowledge. This vibrant atmosphere provided an ideal setting for Falun Gong to emerge and thrive.

Falun Gong distinguished itself during this period through its emphasis on spirituality and moral cultivation. While many qigong systems focused exclusively on physical health, Falun Gong offered a holistic approach that integrated ethical principles with physical exercises. This dual focus resonated with practitioners seeking more than just fitness, attracting a devoted following.

The movement's accessibility also contributed to its growth. Unlike some qigong practices that required formal memberships or fees, Falun Gong was freely available to anyone willing to learn. This openness, combined with the simplicity of its exercises, made it appealing to people of all ages and backgrounds. Practitioners often described the practice as both transformative and empowering, fueling its rapid expansion.

As the Qigong Boom reached its peak, Falun Gong became one of the most prominent practices in China. Its influence extended beyond individual health, inspiring conversations about the intersection of tradition, modernity, and spirituality. The movement's success during this period laid the groundwork for its international spread, ensuring that its impact would extend far beyond its origins in China.

LI HONGZHI AND THE ESTABLISHMENT OF FALUN GONG

EARLY LIFE AND INSPIRATIONS OF LI HONGZHI

Li Hongzhi's early years remain a fascinating puzzle, often framed by both myth and fact. Born in 1951 in Gongzhuling, Jilin Province, his childhood was reportedly steeped in tales of spiritual mentors and unexplainable abilities. Stories abound of his encounters with enlightened teachers who supposedly guided his understanding of energy and the universe. For followers, these accounts solidify his role as a figure of profound insight, though skeptics often raise an eyebrow at their lack of verification.

Growing up in a rapidly modernizing China, Li's formative years coincided with significant cultural shifts. Traditional beliefs were being challenged, but pockets of ancient practices like Daoist alchemy and Buddhist meditation persisted. Whether through familial connections or sheer curiosity, Li is said to have delved into these teachings, finding resonance in their promises of spiritual elevation. It's worth noting that China's cultural context in the mid-20th century was one where such pursuits often remained hidden from public scrutiny.

As an adult, Li worked in ordinary professions, including as a trumpet player and a clerk, before stepping into his eventual role as the founder of Falun Gong. These seemingly mundane roles contrast sharply with the larger-than-life figure he would later become. Followers often point to this contrast as evidence of his humility, a quality they believe underscores the authenticity of his teachings.

Accounts of his inspirations are dotted with anecdotes that border on the fantastical. From reportedly practicing advanced meditative techniques at an early age to claims of healing abilities, Li's life story often toes the line between biography and legend. For his supporters, these elements are not exaggerations but reflections of a man whose understanding of the universe transcends conventional limits.

While his personal journey remains a topic of debate, Li Hongzhi's early years undeniably set the stage for his later role as the leader of a movement that would captivate millions. Whether one views him as a spiritual prodigy or a figure shrouded in self-crafted mystique, his path to founding Falun Gong was anything but ordinary.

FOUNDING OF FALUN GONG IN 1992

In 1992, Li Hongzhi introduced Falun Gong to the world during a public lecture in Changchun, China. This event marked the official beginning of what would become a global spiritual movement. The timing was crucial; China was experiencing a surge of interest in qigong practices, and Li's blend of physical exercises and moral teachings struck a chord with the public. From the outset, Falun Gong distinguished itself with its emphasis on spiritual cultivation over physical prowess.

The initial gatherings were modest, often held in community centers or parks. Li's teachings quickly gained traction, attracting individuals from diverse walks of life. Unlike many contemporary qigong practices, Falun Gong did not require fees or formal memberships, which added to its appeal. People flocked to hear Li speak, intrigued by his clear explanations of profound concepts and his ability to connect ancient traditions with modern-day challenges.

Li's approach was systematic yet accessible. He outlined a series of exercises that were simple to learn but deeply impactful, paired with teachings that emphasized truthfulness, compassion, and forbearance. This combination of physical and spiritual guidance created a framework that resonated with people seeking more than just health benefits. For many, Falun Gong offered a path to personal transformation.

The year 1992 also marked the beginning of Falun Gong's rapid expansion. Word spread quickly, fueled by glowing testimonials from practitioners who credited the practice with improved health and newfound purpose. Local practice groups sprouted across China, creating a grassroots network that operated with remarkable efficiency despite the lack of formal hierarchy.

By the mid-1990s, Falun Gong had grown from a niche practice to a nationwide phenomenon. Its rise was a testament to both the universality of its teachings and the magnetic appeal of Li Hongzhi. Whether viewed as a spiritual revolution or a cultural movement, the founding of Falun Gong in 1992 was a moment that forever altered the landscape of Qigong and beyond.

KEY TEACHINGS OF THE MASTER

Li Hongzhi's teachings are at the heart of Falun Gong, shaping both its philosophical framework and practical exercises. Central to his message are three core principles: truthfulness, compassion, and forbearance. These values are not mere abstract ideals but are presented as actionable guidelines for everyday life. Practitioners are encouraged to embody these virtues in their thoughts, words, and actions, believing that doing so aligns them with the universe's fundamental truths.

One of Li's key teachings is the idea of karma and virtue. Karma is described as a form of negative energy accumulated through bad deeds, while virtue is its positive counterpart, earned through good actions. According to Li, karma can manifest as illness or misfortune, and the cultivation of virtue is essential for overcoming life's challenges. This perspective frames morality not just as a social construct but as a tangible force influencing one's well-being.

Another prominent aspect of Li's teachings is the concept of self-cultivation. He emphasizes the importance of looking inward, identifying attachments and negative habits, and striving for continuous improvement. This process is seen as the key to both personal and spiritual growth. For practitioners, self-cultivation is not a one-time effort but a lifelong journey of refinement and discovery.

Li also introduces metaphysical concepts, such as the existence of higher dimensions and the interconnectedness of all life. While these ideas may seem abstract, they are presented in a way that encourages curiosity and exploration. Practitioners are invited to reflect on their place in the universe, using these teachings as a lens through which to view their own experiences.

At its core, Li's philosophy is one of integration. He weaves together elements of traditional Chinese thought, modern existential questions, and universal values, creating a cohesive system that speaks to a wide audience. His teachings serve as both a foundation and a guide, offering a path to understanding oneself and the world at large.

PUBLIC LECTURES AND GLOBAL OUTREACH

Li Hongzhi's public lectures were a driving force behind Falun Gong's early growth and eventual global reach. These events, held in cities across China and later internationally, introduced audiences to the practice's principles and exercises. Delivered with clarity and passion, Li's lectures captivated listeners, many of whom became lifelong practitioners after attending a single session.

The format of these lectures was straightforward yet impactful. Li often began by discussing the philosophical underpinnings of Falun Gong, explaining concepts like karma, virtue, and self-cultivation. He would then demonstrate the exercises, guiding participants through the movements while answering questions from the audience. This interactive approach made the practice feel both accessible and deeply personal.

As Falun Gong gained momentum, Li expanded his outreach beyond China. In the mid-1990s, he began traveling to countries like the United States, Canada, and Australia, introducing the practice to a global audience. These international lectures drew diverse crowds, reflecting the universal appeal of Falun Gong's teachings. For many attendees, Li's ability to bridge cultural and linguistic gaps was a testament to the universality of his message.

The global outreach efforts were further supported by the publication of *Zhuan Falun*, Li's comprehensive guide to the practice. Translated into multiple languages, the book became a cornerstone of Falun Gong, allowing people worldwide to engage with its teachings. Public lectures and *Zhuan Falun* worked in tandem, creating a feedback loop that fueled the practice's rapid expansion.

Li's lectures were more than just informational sessions; they were transformative experiences for many. Attendees often described feeling a sense of clarity and purpose, as if the teachings had unlocked something within them. This ability to inspire and connect on such a profound level was a key factor in Falun Gong's success, both in China and beyond.

THE PHILOSOPHY BEHIND THE PRACTICE

The philosophy of Falun Gong, as outlined by Li Hongzhi, is deeply rooted in the principles of truthfulness, compassion, and forbearance. These three values form the moral backbone of the practice, serving as both a guide for daily life and a path to spiritual enlightenment. For practitioners, embodying these principles is not just a theoretical exercise but a transformative process that impacts every aspect of their existence.

Truthfulness, the first pillar, emphasizes honesty with oneself and others. Li teaches that being truthful extends beyond merely telling the truth; it involves aligning one's thoughts, words, and actions with an unshakable sense of integrity. Practitioners are encouraged to reflect on their own behaviors, identifying and correcting instances where they may have strayed from this principle. This self-awareness is seen as a key step toward personal growth.

Compassion, the second pillar, calls for empathy and kindness in all interactions. Li describes compassion as a universal force that binds humanity, encouraging practitioners to act with generosity and understanding. This principle extends beyond interpersonal relationships, encompassing a broader respect for all life forms. By cultivating compassion, practitioners aim to create harmony within themselves and their communities.

Forbearance, the third pillar, focuses on patience and resilience in the face of challenges. Li teaches that adversity is an opportunity for growth, urging practitioners to endure hardships with grace and dignity. This principle is particularly significant in the context of Falun Gong's history, as followers have often faced societal and political pressures. For many, forbearance is both a personal and collective virtue, embodying the strength of their convictions.

These three principles are not treated as separate entities but as interconnected facets of a holistic philosophy. Practitioners are taught that aligning with these values enhances their moral character, improves their health, and fosters spiritual clarity. The philosophy of Falun Gong, as such, is not just a set of teachings but a way of life, offering a framework for navigating the complexities of the modern world.

Li's emphasis on these principles also sets Falun Gong apart from other practices. While physical exercises and meditation are integral components, the focus on moral and ethical cultivation elevates Falun Gong to a comprehensive system of self-improvement. This philosophical depth has drawn countless individuals to the practice, each seeking a greater understanding of themselves and their place in the universe.

THE DEBATE AROUND HIS PERSONA

Li Hongzhi's persona has been a subject of fascination, admiration, and controversy since the inception of Falun Gong. To his followers, he is a revered teacher and spiritual guide, someone who has unlocked profound truths about the universe. To his critics, he is a polarizing figure whose claims and teachings invite skepticism. This duality has fueled an ongoing debate about the man behind the movement.

Supporters often highlight Li's humility and accessibility as defining traits of his character. Despite his status as the founder of a global movement, he has consistently avoided the trappings of celebrity. Followers describe him as a straightforward and unassuming individual, focused solely on sharing his teachings. This simplicity resonates deeply with practitioners, reinforcing their trust in his message.

Critics, however, point to certain elements of his teachings and public statements as contentious. Li's assertions about higher dimensions, extraterrestrial life, and the nature of karma have drawn scrutiny, with detractors questioning their scientific validity. For skeptics, these claims undermine his credibility, casting doubt on the broader philosophy of Falun Gong.

The debate is further complicated by Li's decision to relocate to the United States in the late 1990s. While some view this move as a practical response to increasing tensions in China, others interpret it as an attempt to evade scrutiny. The relocation also shifted the narrative surrounding Falun Gong, positioning Li as both a leader in exile and a figure of controversy on the international stage.

For practitioners, these debates often fade in the face of their personal experiences. Many credit Li's teachings with profound transformations in their health, character, and outlook on life. These testimonials serve as a counterbalance to external criticisms, highlighting the deep connection between Li and his followers.

Li Hongzhi's persona, like Falun Gong itself, is complex and multifaceted. Whether seen as a visionary, a teacher, or a polarizing figure, his influence on the movement is undeniable. The debates surrounding him are not merely about the man but about the broader questions of faith, truth, and the nature of belief in the modern age.

LEGACY AND LEADERSHIP

Li Hongzhi's legacy is intricately tied to the enduring impact of Falun Gong, a movement that has transcended its origins to become a global phenomenon. As the founder and spiritual leader, his influence is felt not only through his teachings but also through the community he has nurtured. For practitioners, Li's leadership embodies the principles of truthfulness, compassion, and forbearance, serving as a model for their own journeys.

One of the most notable aspects of Li's leadership is his hands-off approach. Unlike traditional religious or spiritual leaders who maintain centralized control, Li has fostered a decentralized network of practitioners. This structure allows for organic growth and adaptability, with local groups operating independently while staying connected through shared teachings. For followers, this autonomy reinforces their sense of personal responsibility within the practice.

Li's role as a leader extends beyond the philosophical. In the face of persecution, he has become a symbol of resilience and courage. The Chinese government's crackdown on Falun Gong in the late 1990s brought unprecedented challenges to the movement, yet Li's steadfastness has inspired practitioners to remain committed. His emphasis on forbearance has resonated deeply, providing a moral framework for navigating adversity.

The legacy of Falun Gong also includes its contributions to global conversations about human rights and freedom of belief. Li's leadership has elevated the movement's visibility, drawing attention to issues that transcend the practice itself. For many, Falun Gong represents not just a spiritual path but a broader commitment to principles of justice and dignity.

As the movement continues to evolve, Li's teachings remain a cornerstone of its identity. His writings, particularly *Zhuan Falun*, are studied and revered by practitioners worldwide, ensuring that his philosophy endures. Whether viewed as a spiritual pioneer or a controversial figure, Li Hongzhi's legacy continues to shape the lives of millions, leaving an indelible mark on both the practice and the world.

THE CORE PRINCIPLES OF FALUN GONG

TRUTHFULNESS (ZHEN)

Truthfulness is the cornerstone of Falun Gong's philosophy, serving as the first of its three guiding principles. This value goes beyond the simple act of telling the truth; it demands an unwavering commitment to authenticity in thought, word, and deed. Practitioners are encouraged to reflect deeply on their lives, identifying areas where dishonesty, even in its most subtle forms, may have crept in. It's a principle that holds up a mirror to one's inner world and asks for brutal honesty, not just with others but with oneself.

The practice of truthfulness is woven into daily interactions. Whether it's a casual conversation or a critical decision, practitioners aim to embody sincerity and clarity. Li Hongzhi teaches that truthfulness isn't about being blunt or hurtful but about aligning one's actions with an inner moral compass. This approach creates a harmony that practitioners believe resonates outward, influencing relationships and communities.

Adhering to truthfulness often requires a reevaluation of personal habits and societal norms. In a world where white lies and half-truths are often considered harmless or even necessary, Falun Gong challenges these conventions. Practitioners find themselves questioning common practices, like bending the truth to avoid conflict or exaggerating achievements to gain favor. For many, this reevaluation leads to profound personal growth.

This principle also extends to one's inner dialogue. Practitioners are taught to identify self-deception, those little stories we tell ourselves to justify bad habits or avoid difficult truths. By confronting these narratives, they strive for a state of clarity and authenticity that aligns with the universe's natural order. Truthfulness, in this sense, becomes a tool for both moral and spiritual refinement.

The commitment to truthfulness often comes with challenges. Practitioners may face misunderstandings or resistance from those who don't share their values. Yet, they view these difficulties as opportunities to strengthen their resolve and deepen their practice. By embodying truthfulness, they believe they are not only improving themselves but also contributing to a more honest and harmonious world.

COMPASSION (SHAN)

Compassion is at the heart of Falun Gong's teachings, representing the principles of kindness and empathy. It's not merely about being nice to others; it's a profound commitment to understanding and alleviating suffering, both in oneself and in the world. This principle challenges practitioners to look beyond surface interactions and engage with others on a deeper, more meaningful level.

The practice of compassion begins with mindfulness. Practitioners are taught to observe their thoughts and actions, identifying moments when they may have acted out of selfishness or anger. By cultivating awareness, they aim to replace negative tendencies with positive ones, transforming their interactions into opportunities for connection and healing. This process is seen as a continuous journey rather than a fixed state.

Compassion in Falun Gong is not limited to interpersonal relationships. It extends to all living beings, reflecting a belief in the interconnectedness of life. Practitioners often speak of developing a sense of universal love, one that transcends cultural, social, and even species boundaries. This expansive view of compassion inspires acts of service and kindness that go beyond the immediate circle of family and friends.

One of the unique aspects of this principle is its application during moments of adversity. Practitioners are encouraged to respond to hostility or criticism with patience and understanding, seeing these situations as tests of their commitment to compassion. This approach requires not only empathy but also a strong sense of self-discipline, as it often goes against natural instincts to retaliate or defend oneself.

The cultivation of compassion also brings a sense of fulfillment and purpose. Many practitioners describe feeling a deep connection to the world around them as if their acts of kindness create ripples that extend far beyond their immediate surroundings. For them, compassion is not just a principle but a way of life, one that enriches their existence and inspires those around them.

FORBEARANCE (REN)

Forbearance, or *Ren*, is the practice of patience and resilience in the face of challenges. It is perhaps the most demanding of Falun Gong's principles, requiring practitioners to maintain composure and dignity during moments of hardship. This value is not about passivity or resignation but about cultivating inner strength and grace, even when the odds seem insurmountable.

Practitioners often describe forbearance as a test of their character. Life, they believe, presents countless opportunities to practice this principle, from minor irritations to major crises. Whether it's dealing with a difficult colleague or navigating a personal loss, they aim to respond with calm and understanding. This approach is seen as a way to transcend the immediate situation and grow as individuals.

Forbearance also plays a critical role in conflict resolution. Practitioners are encouraged to avoid escalating tensions and instead focus on finding peaceful solutions. This mindset challenges the reactive tendencies that often fuel disputes, promoting a more thoughtful and measured approach. In this sense, forbearance becomes a tool for fostering harmony, both internally and externally.

The principle is especially significant in the context of Falun Gong's history. As practitioners have faced persecution and discrimination, forbearance has served as a guiding light, helping them navigate these trials with courage and integrity. Many describe their commitment to *Ren* as a source of empowerment, enabling them to endure hardships without compromising their values.

Practicing forbearance often leads to a deeper sense of self-awareness and perspective. By stepping back from immediate emotions and reactions, practitioners find clarity and balance. This shift in mindset allows them to approach life's challenges with renewed strength, turning obstacles into opportunities for growth and transformation.

INTEGRATION WITH PERSONAL MORALITY

Falun Gong emphasizes the integration of its principles into every aspect of life, particularly personal morality. This means that truthfulness, compassion, and forbearance are not just abstract ideals but practical guidelines for daily living. Practitioners are encouraged to align their actions with these values, creating a cohesive and authentic way of being.

This integration begins with self-reflection. Practitioners are taught to examine their thoughts, words, and behaviors, identifying areas where they may fall short of the practice's principles. This process is not about self-criticism but about cultivating a genuine desire for improvement. By addressing these gaps, they aim to create a life that is both ethical and fulfilling.

Personal morality also extends to one's interactions with others. Practitioners strive to be honest, kind, and patient, even in challenging situations. This commitment often leads to stronger relationships and a deeper sense of trust and respect from those around them. For many, the practice becomes a way to inspire and uplift others through their own example.

The integration of morality is not limited to major life decisions; it also applies to the small, everyday choices that shape one's character. Whether it's returning a lost wallet, offering a kind word, or simply listening without judgment, these acts of integrity reinforce the practice's principles. Over time, they become second nature, creating a seamless connection between belief and behavior.

This approach to morality also encourages practitioners to take responsibility for their actions. By acknowledging their mistakes and striving to make amends, they embody the practice's emphasis on accountability and growth. This process not only strengthens their character but also deepens their understanding of Falun Gong's teachings.

THE ROLE OF KARMA IN DAILY LIFE

In Falun Gong, karma is seen as a fundamental force that shapes one's experiences and circumstances. It is described as the accumulation of negative actions and thoughts, which manifest as obstacles or suffering. Practitioners believe that by cultivating virtue and aligning with the practice's principles, they can reduce their karma and create a more harmonious life.

Karma is often viewed as a teacher, offering lessons about the consequences of one's actions. Practitioners are encouraged to approach challenges with this perspective, seeing them as opportunities for growth rather than as punishments. This mindset fosters resilience and a sense of purpose, transforming difficulties into stepping stones on the path to spiritual development.

The practice of reducing karma involves both action and intention. Practitioners strive to act with integrity, kindness, and patience, creating positive energy that counterbalances their past misdeeds. This process is seen as an ongoing journey, one that requires constant mindfulness and effort.

Karma also influences how practitioners view their interactions with others. They are taught to approach conflicts with understanding, recognizing that these situations may be tied to karmic connections. By responding with compassion and forbearance, they aim to resolve these ties and create positive relationships.

This understanding of karma extends beyond the individual, highlighting the interconnectedness of all life. Practitioners believe that their actions contribute to a collective balance, influencing not just their own lives but the world around them. This perspective inspires a sense of responsibility and encourages acts of kindness that ripple outward, creating a more harmonious society.

SPIRITUAL ASCENSION THROUGH PRACTICE

Spiritual ascension is a central goal in Falun Gong, seen as the natural outcome of embodying its principles of truthfulness, compassion, and forbearance. Practitioners believe that through disciplined practice, they can purify their minds, shed negative attachments, and align with the universe's higher truths. This journey is deeply personal, requiring both introspection and action to cultivate inner transformation.

The concept of spiritual ascension is closely tied to self-cultivation. Practitioners are encouraged to examine their thoughts and behaviors, identifying attachments such as greed, jealousy, and resentment. These attachments are seen as barriers to spiritual growth, and overcoming them is viewed as a critical step on the path to enlightenment. This process is not about perfection but about consistent effort to elevate one's character.

Meditation and physical exercises play a key role in this ascension. These practices are designed to harmonize the body and mind, creating a state of clarity and focus that supports spiritual development. The exercises are seen not just as physical movements but as expressions of the practice's deeper principles. Practitioners often describe a sense of inner peace and heightened awareness during and after these sessions.

Ascension is also understood as a shift in perspective. Practitioners strive to see beyond the material world, focusing instead on spiritual truths and universal principles. This perspective encourages a sense of detachment from superficial concerns, fostering a deeper connection to the self and the cosmos. For many, this shift brings a profound sense of purpose and fulfillment.

The journey of spiritual ascension is both challenging and rewarding. It requires patience, resilience, and a willingness to confront one's flaws. Yet, practitioners often speak of the profound joy and clarity they experience as they progress. For them, spiritual ascension is not just a destination but a way of living that brings meaning and harmony to their lives.

BALANCING MATERIAL AND SPIRITUAL GOALS

One of the unique aspects of Falun Gong is its emphasis on balancing material and spiritual pursuits. Practitioners are encouraged to live in the world while maintaining a focus on their spiritual development. This balance reflects the practice's holistic approach, which integrates personal growth with everyday life.

Material goals, such as career success and financial stability, are not seen as inherently negative in Falun Gong. Instead, they are viewed as opportunities to practice the principles of truthfulness, compassion, and forbearance. For example, a practitioner might approach their work with integrity, treat colleagues with kindness, and handle challenges with patience. These actions align with the practice's values while contributing to material success.

At the same time, practitioners are taught to avoid becoming overly attached to material pursuits. Excessive focus on wealth, status, or possessions can distract from spiritual growth and create unnecessary stress. Falun Gong encourages a mindset of moderation, where material goals are pursued responsibly but do not overshadow the importance of inner development.

This balance extends to relationships and personal responsibilities. Practitioners strive to embody the practice's principles in their roles as family members, friends, and community members. By doing so, they create harmony in their relationships while deepening their spiritual practice. This integration of values and actions fosters a sense of coherence and authenticity in their lives.

Balancing material and spiritual goals often involves navigating societal pressures and expectations. Practitioners may face challenges in maintaining their principles in environments that prioritize competition or superficial success. Yet, these challenges are seen as opportunities to strengthen their commitment and refine their practice. By achieving this balance, practitioners aim to create lives that are both meaningful and aligned with the practice's teachings.

THE PRACTICE OF FALUN GONG

INTRODUCTION TO THE FIVE EXERCISES

The physical practice of Falun Gong centers around five distinct exercises, each designed to harmonize the body and mind while fostering spiritual growth. These exercises, simple yet profound, combine gentle movements with a meditative focus. Practitioners perform them in a quiet environment, often accompanied by soft music that guides the rhythm of the routines. The five exercises are sequential, building on one another to create a holistic experience that balances physical energy and mental clarity.

The first exercise, "Buddha Stretching a Thousand Arms," involves a series of slow, deliberate stretches. These movements aim to open up the body's energy channels, releasing tension and promoting flexibility. Practitioners describe this exercise as invigorating yet calming, as it encourages a heightened awareness of the body. Each stretch is intentional, emphasizing control and mindfulness over brute force or speed.

The second and third exercises are standing meditations that involve holding various poses for extended periods. These postures are designed to strengthen the body while cultivating patience and inner focus. Practitioners often experience an initial discomfort, but as they persist, the poses become more manageable. This process is seen as symbolic of the practice's broader teachings, highlighting the value of perseverance and self-discipline.

The fourth exercise, "Falun Cosmic Orbit," incorporates smooth, circular movements that mimic the natural flow of energy within the body. Practitioners visualize this energy circulating, creating a sensation of warmth and vitality. The movements are repetitive yet soothing, allowing the mind to settle into a meditative state while the body moves with fluidity and grace.

The fifth and final exercise is a seated meditation that focuses on stillness and deep concentration. Practitioners cross their legs in the lotus or half-lotus position, close their eyes, and rest their hands in a symbolic mudra. This exercise is considered the most spiritually profound, as it invites practitioners to quiet the mind and connect with higher dimensions of existence. Together, these five exercises form the physical foundation of Falun Gong, blending movement and meditation into a unified practice.

THE MEDITATIVE FOCUS OF FALUN GONG

Meditation in Falun Gong is not just an exercise for the mind; it is a gateway to profound spiritual transformation.

The practice emphasizes stillness and introspection, allowing practitioners to quiet their thoughts and align with universal principles. Unlike other meditative practices that focus solely on mindfulness, Falun Gong meditation integrates its core values—truthfulness, compassion, and forbearance—into the experience.

The act of sitting in meditation begins with a deliberate choice to step away from the distractions of daily life. Practitioners find a quiet space, often outdoors or in a calm room, and prepare themselves mentally and physically. The process is not about escaping reality but about engaging with it from a deeper perspective. This distinction sets Falun Gong's meditation apart, as it encourages active reflection alongside the stillness.

Breathing is an essential component of meditation, though it is not as strictly regulated as in some other practices. Practitioners are encouraged to let their breath flow naturally, using it as an anchor for their focus. This simplicity allows them to ease into a state of calm without feeling constrained by rigid techniques. The emphasis is on being present and open rather than achieving a specific state of mind.

Visualization often plays a role during meditation. Practitioners may imagine energy flowing through their bodies or visualize themselves embodying the practice's core values. These mental exercises are not meant to distract but to enhance the meditative experience, creating a sense of connection between the physical and the spiritual. The visuals serve as a reminder of the practice's purpose, grounding the experience in its principles.

The meditative focus of Falun Gong extends beyond the formal exercises. Practitioners aim to carry this sense of mindfulness and alignment into their daily lives. By fostering a meditative mindset, they find themselves better equipped to navigate challenges and maintain a sense of inner peace, no matter the circumstances.

PHYSICAL AND SPIRITUAL BENEFITS

The benefits of practicing Falun Gong are often described as transformative, encompassing both physical health and spiritual well-being. On a physical level, the exercises are designed to improve circulation, enhance flexibility, and reduce stress. Practitioners frequently report feeling lighter and more energized after a session, attributing these changes to the unblocking of energy channels within the body.

Beyond the physical, the spiritual benefits of Falun Gong are equally compelling. Practitioners believe that aligning with the principles of truthfulness, compassion, and forbearance enhances their character and fosters a sense of inner peace. This alignment is not merely theoretical; it manifests in tangible ways, such as improved relationships and a greater sense of purpose. Many describe feeling more connected to themselves and to the world around them.

The combination of physical and spiritual practices also impacts mental health. The meditative exercises help to calm the mind, reducing anxiety and promoting focus. Practitioners often find themselves more patient and resilient, better able to handle life's ups and downs. These mental shifts are seen as a reflection of the practice's deeper teachings, which emphasize self-awareness and growth.

One unique aspect of Falun Gong is its focus on long-term benefits rather than immediate gratification. While the physical exercises provide an instant sense of relaxation, the spiritual and emotional changes unfold gradually. Practitioners view this slow transformation as a testament to the practice's depth, as it requires consistent effort and reflection.

The benefits of Falun Gong extend beyond the individual. Practitioners often share stories of how their practice has positively influenced their families and communities. By embodying the principles of the practice, they create a ripple effect that inspires others to strive for greater harmony and understanding.

CREATING A DAILY PRACTICE ROUTINE

Establishing a daily routine is essential for integrating Falun Gong into one's life. The practice is designed to be adaptable, allowing practitioners to tailor their routines to fit their schedules and needs. Whether performed in the morning, evening, or throughout the day, the exercises and meditative practices provide a consistent anchor in a world that often feels chaotic.

The first step in creating a routine is finding a dedicated space for practice. This could be a corner of a room, a garden, or a local park. The environment should be quiet and free from distractions, allowing practitioners to focus fully on their exercises. For many, this space becomes a sanctuary, a place where they can retreat from the demands of daily life and reconnect with themselves.

Time management is another critical aspect. Practitioners are encouraged to set aside time each day for their practice, even if it's just 20 minutes. Consistency is more important than duration, as regular practice creates a rhythm that reinforces the benefits. Some practitioners prefer shorter sessions throughout the day, while others dedicate a longer block of time to their exercises and meditation.

The sequence of the five exercises provides a natural structure for the routine. Practitioners often begin with the first exercise to warm up their bodies and gradually progress through the sequence. This flow creates a sense of continuity as each exercise builds on the previous one. For those who are pressed for time, focusing on one or two exercises can still yield significant benefits.

Incorporating the principles of truthfulness, compassion, and forbearance into the routine is equally important. Practitioners are encouraged to reflect on these values during their practice, using the time as an opportunity for self-improvement. This integration transforms the routine from a physical exercise into a holistic experience, enriching both the body and the mind.

THE ROLE OF GROUP PRACTICE

Group practice holds a special place in Falun Gong, offering practitioners a sense of community and shared purpose. While the practice can be done individually, gathering with others creates a dynamic energy that enhances the experience. Parks, community centers, and private homes often serve as meeting spaces where practitioners come together to perform the exercises and discuss the teachings.

The benefits of group practice extend beyond the exercises themselves. Practicing in a group fosters a sense of accountability, as practitioners are more likely to stay consistent when they know others are depending on them. It also provides an opportunity to learn from more experienced practitioners who can offer guidance and corrections to improve technique.

Group practice also creates a supportive environment for reflection and growth. Practitioners often share their experiences and insights, creating a space for dialogue and mutual encouragement. These interactions deepen their understanding of the practice and reinforce their commitment to its principles. The sense of belonging that emerges from these gatherings is often described as one of the most rewarding aspects of the practice.

The communal aspect of group practice also amplifies its meditative focus. The collective energy of the group enhances the sense of calm and concentration, making it easier for individuals to enter a meditative state. This shared energy is seen as a reflection of the interconnectedness of life, a core concept in Falun Gong.

Group practice is not just a physical gathering but a symbolic act of unity. It represents the collective effort to embody truthfulness, compassion, and forbearance, creating a ripple effect that extends beyond the group. For many practitioners, these gatherings are a reminder of the power of community and the shared journey of self-cultivation.

CHALLENGES IN DEVELOPING CONSISTENCY

Developing consistency in practicing Falun Gong is often one of the biggest hurdles practitioners face. Modern life, with its endless stream of obligations, distractions, and unexpected events, can make it difficult to establish and maintain a routine. Practitioners often speak of their initial struggles to carve out time, balance priorities, and remain committed to the practice amidst life's demands.

One common challenge is the mental resistance to forming new habits. Practitioners may start with enthusiasm, only to find their motivation waning as the novelty wears off. This phenomenon is familiar to anyone who has ever tried to stick to a fitness or wellness routine. The teachings of Falun Gong encourage practitioners to see these moments not as failures but as opportunities to strengthen their resolve and learn about their own patterns of procrastination or avoidance.

External factors, such as work, family responsibilities, and social obligations, can also pose challenges. Practitioners may struggle to find uninterrupted time or a quiet space for their exercises and meditation. Some respond by adapting their routines, breaking sessions into shorter segments or practicing during less busy times of the day. These adjustments reflect the flexibility of the practice, which can be tailored to fit diverse lifestyles.

Another obstacle is the occasional sense of stagnation or lack of progress. Practitioners might feel that their practice has become repetitive or that the benefits they initially experienced have plateaued. The teachings of Falun Gong address this by emphasizing the importance of continuous self-reflection and growth. Practitioners are encouraged to revisit the principles of truthfulness, compassion, and forbearance, using them as a lens to evaluate their challenges and refine their approach.

Despite these difficulties, practitioners often find that persistence pays off. Small, consistent efforts accumulate, creating a sense of momentum and fulfillment. Many describe their eventual breakthroughs as deeply rewarding, not just for the physical and spiritual benefits but also for the sense of discipline and self-mastery they develop. These experiences highlight the practice's capacity to foster resilience and adaptability, even in the face of life's inevitable obstacles.

THE IMPACT OF PRACTICE ON HEALTH

The health benefits of Falun Gong have been a recurring theme among practitioners, many of whom credit the practice with profound improvements in their physical and mental well-being. While scientific studies on Falun Gong remain limited, the anecdotes from practitioners offer compelling evidence of its transformative effects. These accounts range from reduced stress and anxiety to remarkable recoveries from chronic conditions.

One of the primary health benefits cited is stress relief. The combination of slow, deliberate movements and meditative focus creates a calming effect on the mind and body. Practitioners often report feeling more relaxed and centered after their sessions, describing a sense of lightness that carries over into their daily lives. This reduction in stress can have cascading effects, improving sleep quality, mood, and overall resilience.

The physical exercises also contribute to improved health by promoting circulation, flexibility, and energy flow. Practitioners frequently describe feeling more energized and less fatigued, even after long or challenging days. The gentle nature of the movements makes them accessible to individuals of all ages and fitness levels, offering a low-impact way to enhance physical vitality.

Mental health benefits are another significant aspect of the practice. The emphasis on self-reflection and alignment with core principles fosters a sense of purpose and clarity. Practitioners often speak of reduced anxiety, heightened focus, and a more positive outlook on life. These changes are not just about feeling better in the moment; they represent a deeper shift in how practitioners approach challenges and relationships.

Many practitioners also attribute their improved health to the spiritual dimensions of Falun Gong. By embodying truthfulness, compassion, and forbearance, they believe they are aligning with universal principles that enhance their well-being. This holistic approach, which integrates physical, mental, and spiritual elements, creates a sense of harmony that practitioners describe as life-changing.

The impact of Falun Gong on health extends beyond individual practitioners. Families, communities, and even workplaces have reported benefits from the ripple effects of the practice. Practitioners who embody the principles of the practice often inspire those around them to adopt healthier, more balanced lifestyles. This collective influence underscores the potential of Falun Gong to create a broader culture of well-being and mindfulness.

ZHUAN FALUN: THE CENTRAL TEXT

STRUCTURE AND ORGANIZATION OF *ZHUAN FALUN*

Zhuan Falun, the cornerstone text of Falun Gong, is structured as a series of nine lectures that systematically lay out the principles, philosophies, and practices of the movement. Each lecture builds on the last, creating a layered approach that guides readers from basic concepts to deeper spiritual insights. The book's format reflects its origins in Li Hongzhi's public teachings, where he addressed both curious newcomers and seasoned practitioners in a way that was accessible yet profound.

The text opens with a foundational discussion of moral character and the importance of self-cultivation. This sets the tone for the rest of the book, establishing that spiritual growth is rooted in aligning one's behavior with universal principles. The chapters then weave through topics ranging from karma and virtue to the nature of the universe, blending philosophical ideas with practical guidance for daily life.

Each lecture is written in a conversational style, mirroring the way Li spoke to his audience. His tone is direct yet approachable, with frequent use of metaphors and anecdotes to clarify complex ideas. This style makes the text engaging and relatable, even when it dives into abstract concepts. Readers often describe feeling as though the book is speaking directly to them, challenging their assumptions and encouraging introspection.

The organization of *Zhuan Falun* allows for repeated reading and reflection. Its layered structure means that new insights often emerge with each pass through the text as readers bring their evolving understanding to bear on its teachings. This dynamic quality has made it a living document for practitioners, one that grows and changes alongside them.

Despite its complexity, the book maintains a sense of coherence and unity. Its structure mirrors the journey of self-cultivation itself: a gradual unfolding of truths that deepens as one progresses. This intentional design has contributed to *Zhuan Falun*'s reputation as a guide not just for practice but for life, offering something of value to readers at every stage of their spiritual journey.

KEY CONCEPTS EXPLAINED

At the heart of *Zhuan Falun* are the principles of truthfulness, compassion, and forbearance, which serve as the foundation for both personal growth and universal harmony. These values are not just philosophical ideals but actionable guidelines woven into every aspect of the text. Li Hongzhi presents them as the keys to aligning with the cosmos, fostering both individual and collective transformation.

The concept of karma plays a significant role in the text, described as the accumulation of negative energy from bad deeds. This energy is believed to manifest as illness, misfortune, or obstacles in life. Conversely, virtue, which arises from good deeds and moral behavior, is portrayed as a source of blessings and opportunities. The interplay between karma and virtue underscores the importance of personal responsibility in shaping one's destiny.

Another central idea is self-cultivation, the process of refining one's character and shedding attachments to worldly desires. This practice is framed as both an internal and external endeavor, requiring introspection and disciplined action. Li emphasizes that true spiritual progress involves facing challenges and learning from them, transforming adversity into opportunities for growth.

The text also introduces the concept of higher dimensions, suggesting that the physical world is only one layer of a much larger, interconnected reality. Li describes these dimensions as accessible through spiritual cultivation, offering glimpses into the deeper workings of the universe. While these ideas may seem esoteric, they are presented in a way that invites curiosity rather than confusion.

Finally, *Zhuan Falun* addresses the balance between spiritual and material life. Li teaches that while practitioners should strive for spiritual elevation, they must also fulfill their earthly responsibilities. This dual focus reflects the holistic nature of Falun Gong, which seeks to harmonize the physical, mental, and spiritual aspects of existence.

THE UNIVERSE, TIME, AND SPACE IN FALUN GONG

One of the more intriguing aspects of *Zhuan Falun* is its exploration of the universe, time, and space. Li Hongzhi presents a vision of reality that transcends traditional scientific understanding, blending metaphysical concepts with spiritual principles. For practitioners, these ideas are not just theoretical musings but integral to their understanding of their place in the cosmos.

Li describes the universe as a vast, layered structure, with each dimension governed by its own set of laws. The physical world, as we perceive it, is merely one layer among many, and spiritual cultivation allows individuals to access higher dimensions. These layers are interconnected, influencing one another in ways that are both subtle and profound.

Time, according to Li, is not linear but multifaceted. He speaks of different temporal frameworks operating in different dimensions, suggesting that time as we experience it is just one aspect of a more complex reality. This concept challenges conventional notions of cause and effect, inviting practitioners to consider the broader implications of their actions across dimensions.

Space, too, is reimagined in *Zhuan Falun*. Li describes it as fluid and dynamic, capable of bending and shifting in response to spiritual energy. This perspective aligns with the practice's emphasis on energy flow and balance, framing space as both a physical and spiritual construct. For practitioners, this understanding reinforces the interconnectedness of all things.

While these ideas may seem abstract, they are grounded in the practice's core principles. Truthfulness, compassion, and forbearance are presented as the keys to navigating this multidimensional reality, aligning one's energy with the universe's natural order. For many practitioners, this perspective offers a sense of wonder and purpose, inspiring them to approach life with humility and curiosity.

Li's exploration of the universe, time, and space is not meant to replace scientific inquiry but to complement it. He invites readers to question their assumptions and expand their understanding, blending ancient wisdom with modern curiosity. For practitioners, these concepts add depth and richness to their practice, connecting their personal journey to the broader mysteries of existence.

UNDERSTANDING THE LAW WHEEL (FALUN)

The Law Wheel, or *Falun*, is one of the most distinctive symbols in Falun Gong, representing the practice's core teachings and spiritual essence. In *Zhuan Falun*, Li Hongzhi describes the Falun as a dynamic, multidimensional energy mechanism that exists within the body of each practitioner. This concept serves as both a metaphor and a tangible aspect of the practice, bridging the physical and spiritual dimensions.

The Falun is said to rotate continuously, drawing in positive energy and expelling negative influences. Practitioners visualize this rotation during their exercises, believing it aligns their energy with the universe's natural rhythms. This process is seen as both purifying and energizing, fostering physical vitality and spiritual clarity.

Li explains that the Falun is not something practitioners create but something he implants during their cultivation journey. This concept highlights the reciprocal relationship between the teacher and the practitioner, as well as the importance of sincerity and dedication in the practice. The Falun is presented as a gift, a tool for self-cultivation that requires commitment to activate its full potential.

The Law Wheel also serves as a symbolic representation of the practice's principles. Its design incorporates elements of Daoism, Buddhism, and traditional Chinese cosmology, reflecting the practice's roots and philosophical depth. For practitioners, the Falun is both a visual reminder of their values and a guide for their spiritual journey.

Understanding the Falun is not about intellectual mastery but about experiential learning. Practitioners are encouraged to focus on their practice, trusting that their understanding of the Falun will deepen as they progress. This emphasis on experience over explanation reflects the broader teachings of Falun Gong, which prioritize personal transformation over theoretical knowledge.

PRACTICAL TEACHINGS FOR SELF-IMPROVEMENT

Zhuan Falun is more than a spiritual guide; it is also a manual for practical self-improvement. Li Hongzhi's teachings encourage practitioners to scrutinize their thoughts, behaviors, and interactions, not through the lens of guilt or blame but with an eye toward growth. This emphasis on actionable steps transforms the practice from abstract philosophy into a toolkit for navigating everyday life.

One of the key teachings in this regard is the cultivation of mindfulness. Practitioners are taught to be fully present in their actions, whether they are performing the exercises, engaging in conversation, or working through challenges. This mindfulness extends to self-reflection, where they examine their reactions to identify attachments like anger, jealousy, or selfishness. By recognizing these patterns, practitioners can begin to shift their habits and attitudes.

Li also stresses the importance of perseverance. Practitioners are reminded that progress requires consistent effort, even when the results are not immediately visible. This teaching encourages them to view setbacks not as failures but as opportunities to test and strengthen their resolve. The process of overcoming obstacles becomes a cornerstone of self-improvement, reinforcing the practice's emphasis on resilience and forbearance.

Another practical aspect of the teachings involves relationships. Practitioners are encouraged to approach others with truthfulness, compassion, and patience, even in difficult situations. This perspective fosters better communication and deeper connections, as it prioritizes understanding over judgment or conflict. Many practitioners report that these teachings have improved their relationships at home, work, and within their communities.

The focus on self-improvement extends to one's broader environment. Practitioners are encouraged to act with integrity, whether they are fulfilling professional responsibilities, managing finances, or contributing to their communities. These actions are seen as expressions of the practice's principles, creating harmony between the individual and the world around them. For practitioners, self-improvement is not just a personal goal but a way of creating a positive ripple effect that benefits everyone they encounter.

COMMON MISINTERPRETATIONS OF *ZHUAN FALUN*

Zhuan Falun is a complex text, and like any philosophical or spiritual work, it is susceptible to misinterpretation. Some readers, unfamiliar with the context of Falun Gong's teachings or overwhelmed by its metaphysical concepts, may draw conclusions that distort the practice's intentions. Li Hongzhi acknowledges this challenge in his lectures, urging readers to approach the text with an open mind and a willingness to reflect deeply.

One common misinterpretation involves the concept of karma. Critics sometimes misconstrue it as a fatalistic view, suggesting that suffering is deserved or inescapable. In reality, Li presents karma as a dynamic force that can be transformed through virtue and self-cultivation. The emphasis is on taking responsibility for one's actions and actively working to create positive change rather than resigning oneself to hardship.

The discussion of higher dimensions and supernatural phenomena has also sparked misunderstandings. Some readers interpret these concepts as fantastical or pseudoscientific, focusing on the surface descriptions rather than their symbolic or spiritual significance. For practitioners, these ideas are less about literal interpretation and more about exploring the interconnectedness of life and the universe.

Another area of confusion involves the role of the Law Wheel (*Falun*). Some critics have dismissed it as purely symbolic or even superstitious. However, practitioners view it as both a metaphor for the practice's principles and a tangible aspect of their spiritual cultivation. The rotation of the Falun, whether visualized or experienced, is central to their understanding of energy flow and balance.

Misinterpretations can also arise from cultural differences. Concepts rooted in traditional Chinese philosophy, such as *qi* and the interplay of yin and yang, may be unfamiliar or misunderstood by readers from different backgrounds. These cultural nuances require context to fully appreciate their significance within the practice.

Despite these challenges, practitioners often find that engaging with *Zhuan Falun* over time clarifies its teachings. Misinterpretations, rather than hindering their progress, become opportunities to deepen their understanding. By revisiting the text with fresh perspectives and applying its principles in their lives, they move closer to grasping its intended meaning.

ITS IMPACT ON FALUN GONG PRACTITIONERS

The impact of *Zhuan Falun* on practitioners is profound, shaping their perspectives, behaviors, and spiritual journeys. For many, the text serves as a catalyst for transformation, providing not only a framework for personal growth but also a sense of purpose and connection. Its teachings resonate on multiple levels, offering insights that extend far beyond the confines of the book itself.

Practitioners often describe *Zhuan Falun* as a guide to navigating life's challenges. The principles of truthfulness, compassion, and forbearance become touchstones that inform their decisions and interactions. Whether they are facing conflicts, making difficult choices, or reflecting on their actions, the teachings provide a steady compass that points toward harmony and integrity.

The text's emphasis on self-cultivation inspires practitioners to approach life with curiosity and humility. By examining their thoughts and behaviors, they uncover patterns and attachments that may have gone unnoticed. This process of self-discovery is both challenging and rewarding, as it encourages them to confront their weaknesses while celebrating their progress.

The sense of community fostered by *Zhuan Falun* is another significant aspect of its impact. Practitioners often share their experiences and insights, creating a network of support and encouragement. These connections reinforce the practice's principles, as they remind individuals that their personal growth is intertwined with the well-being of others.

For many, the spiritual dimensions of the text are its most transformative element. The exploration of karma, higher dimensions, and the Law Wheel invites practitioners to consider their place in a vast, interconnected universe. This perspective fosters a sense of wonder and gratitude, inspiring them to approach life with reverence and purpose.

The impact of *Zhuan Falun* is not limited to the individual; it extends to families, communities, and even global movements. Practitioners who embody its principles often inspire others to explore the practice, creating a ripple effect that amplifies its influence. For those who embrace its teachings, *Zhuan Falun* is more than a book—it is a lifelong companion on the path to self-cultivation and spiritual fulfillment.

THE ROLE OF FALUN GONG IN MODERN SPIRITUALITY

BRIDGING EASTERN AND WESTERN BELIEFS

Falun Gong occupies a unique position as a spiritual practice that blends ancient Eastern traditions with ideas that resonate with Western audiences. Its roots lie in Chinese culture, drawing from Buddhism, Daoism, and traditional qigong, but its principles are presented in a way that transcends cultural boundaries. For practitioners in the West, Falun Gong feels both familiar and new, an intriguing mix of universal values and profound philosophies.

One way Falun Gong bridges these cultural divides is through its emphasis on universal principles like truthfulness, compassion, and forbearance. These values are not tethered to any specific religion or culture, which makes them accessible to people from all walks of life. Western practitioners often find that these principles align with their own spiritual or ethical beliefs, creating a seamless integration into their lives.

The physical exercises also contribute to its cross-cultural appeal. The gentle movements and meditative focus are reminiscent of yoga, tai chi, and other practices that have gained popularity in the West. This familiarity makes the exercises approachable for those new to Eastern traditions, while the spiritual teachings offer depth for those seeking a more profound connection.

Falun Gong's teachings about karma and self-cultivation also resonate with Western audiences. While the concept of karma originates in Eastern philosophy, its emphasis on personal responsibility and the consequences of one's actions aligns with Western ideas of accountability and moral growth. Practitioners find these teachings to be both practical and transformative, offering a framework for navigating life's challenges.

The practice's ability to bridge Eastern and Western beliefs is a testament to its universality. It speaks to the shared human desire for meaning, connection, and self-improvement, breaking down cultural barriers in the process. For many, Falun Gong serves as a reminder that spirituality is not confined to any one tradition but is a journey that transcends borders and traditions.

CONNECTION TO GLOBAL MOVEMENTS

Falun Gong has found a place within the larger tapestry of global spiritual and social movements. Its emphasis on self-cultivation, ethical living, and mindfulness resonates with trends that prioritize personal growth and holistic well-being. In a world increasingly interconnected by technology and shared challenges, Falun Gong offers a unifying philosophy that connects individuals across continents.

The practice's focus on truthfulness has drawn parallels to movements advocating for transparency and authenticity. Practitioners often find themselves aligned with causes that promote ethical leadership, honesty in communication, and integrity in business. This alignment underscores the relevance of Falun Gong's principles in addressing modern societal issues.

Compassion, another core principle, connects Falun Gong to humanitarian efforts worldwide. Many practitioners channel their spiritual growth into acts of service, supporting initiatives that address poverty, education, and healthcare. These contributions reflect the practice's emphasis on interconnectedness, where personal transformation is seen as a catalyst for positive change in the world.

The principle of forbearance has taken on particular significance in the context of human rights advocacy. Falun Gong's history of resilience in the face of persecution has inspired solidarity from other movements that champion freedom of belief and expression. This shared commitment to dignity and justice has created alliances that amplify the practice's impact on a global scale.

Falun Gong's connection to global movements highlights its adaptability and relevance in a rapidly changing world. It is not just a personal practice but a philosophy that intersects with broader efforts to create a more ethical and compassionate society. For practitioners, these connections add meaning to their journey, reinforcing the idea that their spiritual growth contributes to something much larger.

ADAPTING TRADITIONAL PRACTICES FOR MODERN TIMES

Falun Gong's ability to adapt traditional practices to the realities of modern life is one of its most compelling features. While rooted in ancient Chinese culture, the practice has been reimagined to fit the needs and constraints of a contemporary audience. This balance between tradition and innovation makes it both timeless and accessible, a spiritual practice for the here and now.

One way Falun Gong achieves this is through its simplicity. The exercises are easy to learn and require no special equipment or environment. Practitioners can perform them in a park, a living room, or even during a lunch break, making the practice highly adaptable to busy lifestyles. This flexibility allows individuals to integrate Falun Gong into their daily routines without disrupting their other responsibilities.

The teachings also reflect this adaptability. While they draw on ancient principles, they are presented in a conversational and practical manner that resonates with modern sensibilities. Li Hongzhi's use of metaphors and anecdotes makes complex ideas approachable, encouraging practitioners to reflect on their lives in a way that feels relevant and immediate.

Technology has further expanded Falun Gong's reach. Online resources, including videos, forums, and digital copies of *Zhuan Falun*, make it easier than ever for individuals to access the practice. Practitioners can learn the exercises and teachings at their own pace, connecting with a global community from the comfort of their homes. This digital presence ensures that the practice remains vibrant in an increasingly connected world.

Falun Gong's adaptation to modern times does not dilute its essence. Instead, it enhances its relevance, ensuring that its teachings and exercises remain accessible and meaningful. Practitioners appreciate this balance, as it allows them to engage with an ancient tradition in a way that feels deeply personal and aligned with their contemporary lives.

HOW PRACTITIONERS INCORPORATE FALUN GONG DAILY

For practitioners, Falun Gong is not just a set of exercises or teachings; it is a way of life. Incorporating the practice into daily routines involves more than finding time for meditation or reading *Zhuan Falun*. It is about embodying its principles in every action, decision, and interaction, creating a seamless integration between spiritual practice and everyday existence.

Morning often begins with the five exercises. Practitioners find that starting the day with these movements sets a tone of mindfulness and balance. The exercises are more than physical routines; they are opportunities to center the mind and connect with the practice's principles. This morning ritual creates a sense of grounding that carries through the day.

Throughout their day, practitioners apply the principles of truthfulness, compassion, and forbearance to their interactions. Whether at work, school, or home, they strive to be honest, kind, and patient, using challenges as opportunities for self-reflection and growth. This approach transforms routine activities into acts of cultivation, reinforcing the connection between their inner and outer lives.

Reading or reflecting on *Zhuan Falun* often becomes a part of the daily routine. Practitioners may revisit specific passages or explore new insights, using the text as a guide for navigating their experiences. This practice of reflection deepens their understanding of the teachings, creating a dynamic relationship between the text and their lives.

Evenings often include a second round of meditation or reading, offering a moment of quiet before the day ends. Practitioners describe this time as an opportunity to reset, let go of the day's stresses, and reconnect with the practice. This evening ritual mirrors the morning routine, bookending the day with mindfulness and intention.

For practitioners, the daily incorporation of Falun Gong is not about perfection but about consistency. Each day offers new opportunities to align with its principles, creating a rhythm that supports both spiritual growth and practical living. This integration ensures that the practice remains a living, evolving part of their lives rather than a separate or compartmentalized activity.

RESONANCE WITH UNIVERSAL SPIRITUAL TRUTHS

Falun Gong resonates with universal spiritual truths that transcend specific religions or cultural traditions, appealing to those seeking a deeper understanding of life's meaning. At its core are the principles of truthfulness, compassion, and forbearance—values that have been echoed across spiritual traditions for centuries. This alignment with universal truths gives the practice a timeless quality, connecting it to the broader human quest for purpose and enlightenment.

Truthfulness is a cornerstone of many spiritual teachings, often associated with integrity and authenticity. In Falun Gong, truthfulness extends beyond mere honesty to encompass alignment with the universe's fundamental order. Practitioners find this principle resonates with their inner moral compass, offering a framework for navigating personal and ethical challenges.

Compassion is another universal value that is found in the unique expression of Falun Gong. It is not simply about kindness but about cultivating a deep empathy for all beings. This principle invites practitioners to look beyond their own experiences, fostering a sense of interconnectedness that mirrors the teachings of Buddhism, Christianity, and other traditions. For many, this emphasis on compassion serves as a reminder of their shared humanity.

Forbearance, while less frequently highlighted in global spiritual discourse, is equally significant. It calls for patience and resilience, qualities that are often tested in the face of adversity. Practitioners describe forbearance as a grounding force, helping them navigate life's challenges with grace and dignity. This principle echoes the teachings of Stoicism and other philosophies that emphasize inner strength and equilibrium.

Falun Gong also resonates with the universal desire for self-improvement and spiritual growth. Its teachings encourage practitioners to look inward, identify attachments, and strive for continuous refinement. This process of self-cultivation is reflected in diverse spiritual paths, from the meditative practices of Zen Buddhism to the ethical teachings of Confucianism.

The practice's ability to reflect universal truths makes it accessible to people from all backgrounds, regardless of their religious or cultural affiliations. It speaks to a shared yearning for meaning and connection, offering a spiritual path that feels both deeply personal and universally relevant.

PUBLIC PERCEPTIONS IN A GLOBAL CONTEXT

The global reception of Falun Gong has been shaped by a mix of admiration, misunderstanding, and controversy. For many, the practice is seen as a peaceful spiritual path that promotes physical and emotional well-being. Its emphasis on universal values resonates with those seeking a holistic approach to self-improvement. However, public perceptions have also been influenced by political narratives and cultural differences.

In the West, Falun Gong has often been embraced as a form of alternative spirituality. Its focus on meditation and ethical living aligns with broader wellness trends, making it appealing to those exploring mindfulness and holistic health. Many practitioners credit Falun Gong with transformative changes in their lives, sharing testimonials that highlight its positive impact on their physical and mental well-being.

In China, public perceptions are more complex. While Falun Gong was initially celebrated for its health benefits and alignment with traditional Chinese culture, its growing popularity and philosophical depth eventually drew scrutiny. The Chinese government's subsequent crackdown on the practice has led to conflicting narratives, with state media portraying it as subversive while practitioners and international organizations advocate for its peaceful and transformative nature.

Cultural differences also play a role in shaping perceptions. Concepts like *qi*, karma, and higher dimensions may be unfamiliar or misunderstood in Western contexts, leading some to view Falun Gong as esoteric or overly mystical. Conversely, Western emphasis on individualism and self-expression has influenced how the practice is interpreted and integrated outside of China.

The media has further complicated public perceptions, often presenting polarized views of the practice. Positive portrayals emphasize its spiritual and health benefits, while critical narratives focus on controversies or political implications. This duality reflects the challenges of understanding a multifaceted practice in a world of soundbites and simplified narratives.

Despite these varied perceptions, practitioners often describe a sense of clarity and purpose that transcends public opinion. For them, Falun Gong is not about external validation but about personal transformation and alignment with universal principles. This steadfastness has helped the practice maintain its global presence and impact, even amid shifting cultural and political landscapes.

MAINTAINING PURITY OF THE PRACTICE

Maintaining the purity of Falun Gong's teachings is a central concern for practitioners, especially as the practice has spread globally and adapted to diverse cultural contexts. At its heart is the belief that the principles and exercises should remain true to the teachings outlined in *Zhuan Falun* and Li Hongzhi's lectures. This emphasis on authenticity ensures that the practice retains its transformative power and spiritual depth.

One way practitioners uphold the purity of the practice is by adhering strictly to the original teachings. Unlike some spiritual movements that evolve through reinterpretation or institutional changes, Falun Gong emphasizes the unchanging nature of its core principles. Practitioners are encouraged to study *Zhuan Falun* directly and avoid introducing personal interpretations that might dilute or distort its message.

The decentralized structure of Falun Gong also supports the integrity of the practice. Without formal hierarchies or centralized leadership, the focus remains on the teachings themselves rather than on individuals or organizations. This structure fosters a sense of personal responsibility as practitioners take ownership of their spiritual journey while staying connected to the broader community.

Cultural adaptation is another area where purity is carefully balanced. While Falun Gong's principles are universal, its roots in Chinese culture mean that some aspects may require explanation or contextualization for international audiences. Practitioners strive to share the practice in a way that is accessible yet faithful to its origins, ensuring that its essence is preserved across cultural boundaries.

Challenges to maintaining purity also come from external pressures, including political narratives and media portrayals. Practitioners often face the task of clarifying misconceptions and distinguishing the practice from the controversies that surround it. This requires a commitment to truthfulness and a willingness to engage in dialogue, both of which are seen as extensions of the practice itself.

For practitioners, maintaining the purity of Falun Gong is not about rigidity but about respect for its principles and transformative potential. By staying true to the teachings, they ensure that the practice remains a source of guidance and inspiration for themselves and for future generations. This commitment to authenticity underscores the enduring strength and relevance of Falun Gong in a rapidly changing world.

THE CHINESE GOVERNMENT'S RESPONSE

INITIAL SUPPORT AND PROMOTION

In its early years, Falun Gong was not only tolerated by the Chinese government but actively promoted. The practice gained attention during the early 1990s, a period when traditional qigong was experiencing a resurgence, thanks in part to state-sponsored health initiatives. Government agencies and scientific institutions lauded Falun Gong for its reported health benefits, presenting it as an effective way to reduce healthcare costs and improve public well-being.

At that time, Falun Gong practitioners were a common sight in parks and community centers across China. Public demonstrations of the practice drew large crowds, many of whom were intrigued by the combination of physical exercises and spiritual teachings. Local governments often facilitated these gatherings, granting permits and even providing logistical support. It seemed Falun Gong had found a place within the government's broader efforts to promote national health.

The Chinese Qigong Research Society, a semi-official organization, was among the first to recognize Falun Gong's potential. They endorsed the practice and invited Li Hongzhi to lecture at various events, helping to establish its credibility. For a time, Falun Gong was even featured in state media, with newspapers and television programs highlighting the practice's benefits. Practitioners proudly cited these endorsements as evidence of Falun Gong's legitimacy and effectiveness.

Falun Gong's growing popularity, however, began to raise questions among officials. The practice's emphasis on spiritual cultivation distinguished it from other forms of qigong, challenging the secular framework promoted by the state. While the government initially embraced Falun Gong's focus on morality and health, its spiritual dimensions and grassroots growth were increasingly viewed as potential sources of instability.

The turning point came as Falun Gong's numbers swelled into the millions, surpassing the membership of the Communist Party. What had once been celebrated as a health initiative began to be seen as a challenge to the state's authority. This shift marked the end of the government's support and set the stage for the conflict that would follow.

THE 1999 CRACKDOWN

The Chinese government's response to Falun Gong took a dramatic turn in 1999, transforming from cautious observation to outright suppression. On July 20 of that year, a nationwide campaign was launched to dismantle the practice, marking the beginning of what would become a long and contentious conflict. The government cited concerns about social stability and accused Falun Gong of promoting "superstition" and "anti-scientific" beliefs.

The crackdown was precipitated by an event in April 1999, when more than 10,000 practitioners gathered outside the central government compound in Beijing. The peaceful demonstration was organized to request recognition and an end to growing harassment. While the gathering was orderly and non-violent, it alarmed officials, who saw it as an unprecedented display of grassroots organization. The sheer number of participants underscored Falun Gong's influence and solidified the government's resolve to act.

The campaign against Falun Gong was swift and expansive. Practitioners were arrested en masse, practice sites were dismantled, and the group's materials were confiscated and destroyed. The government declared Falun Gong an illegal organization and established the 610 Office, a special task force dedicated to eradicating the practice. This marked the beginning of a concerted effort to eliminate Falun Gong from public life.

State media played a central role in the crackdown, broadcasting propaganda that portrayed Falun Gong as a dangerous cult. Reports accused the practice of causing psychological harm and even deaths, allegations that practitioners vehemently denied. The media blitz aimed to discredit Falun Gong and justify the government's actions, shaping public opinion against the practice.

The crackdown extended beyond physical suppression to include ideological control. Practitioners were pressured to renounce their beliefs through "re-education" programs, often involving intense psychological and physical coercion. For many, this marked the beginning of years of persecution as the government sought to erase Falun Gong from Chinese society.

KEY EVENTS IN THE SUPPRESSION CAMPAIGN

The suppression of Falun Gong has been marked by a series of key events that reveal the scope and intensity of the campaign. These events illustrate not only the government's determination but also the resilience of practitioners, who have persisted in their efforts to uphold their beliefs despite immense challenges.

One of the earliest and most visible actions was the public book burnings that took place in 1999. Authorities confiscated millions of copies of *Zhuan Falun* and other Falun Gong materials, destroying them in mass demonstrations intended to send a clear message. Images of these burnings, broadcast across state media, symbolized the government's intent to eliminate the practice's influence.

Detentions and arrests escalated rapidly, with thousands of practitioners being sent to detention centers, labor camps, and prisons. Many were subjected to harsh conditions and abuse, with reports of torture emerging from human rights organizations. The government's efforts to suppress Falun Gong extended into surveillance and monitoring, targeting anyone suspected of involvement with the practice.

One of the most controversial aspects of the campaign has been allegations of organ harvesting. Multiple investigative reports have claimed that imprisoned Falun Gong practitioners were used as unwilling organ donors for China's transplant industry. These allegations have been widely condemned by international organizations and governments, though the Chinese government denies them.

Practitioners responded to the suppression with acts of peaceful resistance. One of the most dramatic occurred in 2001, when a group of practitioners unfurled a banner reading "Falun Gong is Good" in Tiananmen Square. The protest was quickly dispersed by police, but it captured global attention, highlighting the lengths practitioners were willing to go to defend their beliefs.

The suppression campaign has had lasting effects on both Falun Gong and Chinese society. While the government's efforts have significantly curtailed public practice, Falun Gong continues to exist underground, with practitioners finding ways to maintain their faith despite the risks. The campaign also sparked widespread debate about freedom of belief and human rights, issues that remain central to Falun Gong's legacy.

MEDIA PORTRAYAL OF FALUN GONG

The Chinese government's media campaign against Falun Gong has been relentless, shaping public perceptions of the practice both domestically and internationally. State-run outlets have painted Falun Gong as a dangerous and destabilizing force, using a combination of fear-mongering and misinformation to justify the suppression campaign. These portrayals stand in stark contrast to the accounts of practitioners, who describe their practice as peaceful and transformative.

One of the primary tactics has been to label Falun Gong as a cult, a term loaded with negative connotations. Government broadcasts have accused the practice of brainwashing its followers and causing psychological harm, often citing fabricated or exaggerated stories. These narratives aim to delegitimize Falun Gong and discourage public sympathy for its practitioners.

Dramatic and often gruesome stories have been a hallmark of the propaganda campaign. Reports of practitioners committing self-harm or harming others have been widely publicized despite questions about their credibility. One of the most infamous examples is the 2001 Tiananmen Square self-immolation incident, which state media claimed involved Falun Gong practitioners. Independent investigations have raised doubts about the official account, but the incident remains a cornerstone of the government's narrative.

Internationally, the Chinese government has used its influence to shape how Falun Gong is perceived outside of China. Diplomatic efforts have included pressuring foreign governments and media outlets to avoid supporting or reporting favorably on the practice. These efforts have created a polarized landscape, with some outlets echoing Chinese propaganda and others taking a more critical stance.

Despite these efforts, Falun Gong has found ways to counter the media narrative. Practitioners have established their own media outlets, such as *The Epoch Times*, to share their perspectives and expose human rights abuses. These platforms have become a vital part of the resistance, challenging the government's portrayal and amplifying the voices of those who continue to practice Falun Gong in the face of persecution.

LEGAL AND SOCIAL RAMIFICATIONS FOR PRACTITIONERS

The crackdown on Falun Gong has brought severe legal and social consequences for practitioners in China. Under the government's campaign, practicing Falun Gong or possessing its materials is treated as a criminal offense, punishable by detention, imprisonment, or forced labor. These legal measures aim not just to punish individuals but to deter others from engaging in the practice.

Practitioners arrested for their beliefs often face harsh conditions in detention. Reports from former detainees describe prolonged interrogations, physical abuse, and psychological pressure to renounce Falun Gong. Labor camps have been used to detain practitioners without trial, a practice enabled by China's now-defunct "re-education through labor" system. Even after this system was officially abolished, detentions of Falun Gong adherents have persisted under other legal pretexts.

The social consequences of practicing Falun Gong are equally severe. Many practitioners have lost their jobs, homes, and social standing due to their association with the practice. Employers and schools, under government pressure, often sever ties with known practitioners. This creates a chilling effect, forcing many to choose between their livelihood and their beliefs.

Family relationships have also been strained by the suppression campaign. Practitioners frequently face pressure from relatives to abandon Falun Gong, as their association with the practice can bring scrutiny to their entire household. This dynamic has caused emotional rifts, isolating practitioners from their support networks.

Legal and social persecution has extended beyond China's borders. Practitioners living abroad have reported surveillance and harassment by individuals linked to the Chinese government. These efforts aim to curtail international advocacy and maintain pressure on practitioners, even in countries with strong protections for freedom of belief.

RESISTANCE AND ADVOCACY BY PRACTITIONERS

Despite the risks, Falun Gong practitioners have demonstrated remarkable resilience and creativity in resisting the suppression campaign. Their efforts range from small, personal acts of defiance to large-scale international advocacy, all aimed at protecting their right to practice and raising awareness about the persecution they face.

Inside China, practitioners have established underground networks to share materials, organize practice sessions, and support one another. These networks often use encrypted communication and other security measures to evade detection. Printing and distributing leaflets exposing government propaganda has become a common form of resistance, with practitioners risking arrest to share their message.

Digital advocacy has also played a critical role in resistance efforts. Practitioners have used tools like VPNs to bypass China's internet censorship and share information with the outside world. Platforms like social media and encrypted messaging apps have allowed them to document human rights abuses and connect with international allies.

Outside of China, practitioners have organized protests, marches, and other public events to raise awareness. Tiananmen Square demonstrations during the early 2000s were among the most visible acts of resistance, drawing global attention to the suppression campaign. More recently, practitioners have used artistic and cultural expressions, such as Shen Yun Performing Arts, to share their stories and celebrate their heritage.

Legal advocacy has also become a significant aspect of the resistance. Practitioners and their supporters have filed lawsuits against Chinese officials accused of orchestrating the suppression, leveraging international human rights laws. These efforts aim to hold individuals accountable and create diplomatic pressure on the Chinese government.

The resistance movement reflects the practice's emphasis on forbearance and truthfulness. Practitioners often describe their advocacy not as retaliation but as a way to uphold their values and shine a light on injustice. This commitment has inspired solidarity from human rights organizations, governments, and individuals around the world, amplifying their cause on a global stage.

ONGOING INTERNATIONAL IMPLICATIONS

The suppression of Falun Gong has had far-reaching implications, influencing China's global relationships and sparking debates about human rights, freedom of belief, and international responsibility. What began as a domestic campaign has evolved into a focal point for broader concerns about China's policies and their impact beyond its borders.

One significant area of concern is the issue of human rights. Falun Gong's persecution has been cited in reports by organizations like Amnesty International and Human Rights Watch, as well as in resolutions by the United Nations and national governments. These reports have drawn attention to the broader pattern of rights violations in China, connecting Falun Gong's suppression to issues such as censorship, forced labor, and arbitrary detention.

International advocacy by practitioners has also shaped global perceptions of China. Protests outside Chinese embassies and cultural events like Shen Yun have highlighted the practice's resilience and exposed the suppression campaign to new audiences. These efforts have raised awareness about Falun Gong while prompting questions about the role of foreign governments and businesses in addressing human rights concerns.

The economic dimension of the suppression has also sparked controversy. Allegations of forced organ harvesting have led some countries to restrict medical tourism to China and review their transplant ethics policies. These measures reflect growing concern about the intersection of human rights and global trade, with Falun Gong serving as a case study for the potential ethical costs of economic engagement with China.

Diplomatic relations have not been immune to the impact of the suppression campaign. Governments and lawmakers advocating for Falun Gong have faced backlash from Chinese officials, who often frame such actions as interference in domestic affairs. This dynamic has created tensions in international forums, complicating efforts to address the issue collaboratively.

The ongoing implications of Falun Gong's suppression underscore the interconnectedness of human rights, politics, and global citizenship. For practitioners and their supporters, the fight for justice is not just about Falun Gong but about defending universal principles that transcend borders. This perspective has transformed the campaign into a global movement, ensuring that its legacy will endure as a symbol of resilience and advocacy for freedom.

THE FALUN GONG DIASPORA

GROWTH OF FALUN GONG COMMUNITIES ABROAD

When Falun Gong faced its harshest repression in China, practitioners around the world began to form tight-knit communities as a way to preserve their practice and support one another. These communities became not only sanctuaries for those fleeing persecution but also hubs of activity for spreading awareness and fostering spiritual growth. As Falun Gong expanded across borders, it established itself as a global movement with roots in nearly every corner of the world.

Many of these communities first formed in countries with established Chinese diasporas, such as the United States, Canada, and Australia. Practitioners who immigrated to these regions brought their experiences and dedication, creating spaces where others could learn about Falun Gong. Parks in cities like New York and Toronto soon mirrored those in pre-1999 China, with practitioners gathering for early morning exercises and meditation.

The growth of these communities wasn't limited to those with Chinese heritage. The universal appeal of Falun Gong's principles—truthfulness, compassion, and forbearance—attracted people from diverse backgrounds. Open practice sessions and public demonstrations introduced the teachings to new audiences, many of whom were drawn to the practice's emphasis on personal growth and ethical living. These multicultural communities became microcosms of the movement's global reach.

Language barriers, though initially a challenge, were overcome with determination. Practitioners translated key texts, including *Zhuan Falun*, into dozens of languages, ensuring that the teachings were accessible to anyone interested. Cultural adaptation also played a role, as practitioners worked to present Falun Gong in a way that resonated with local customs without compromising its core principles.

Despite the distance from China, these communities maintained a deep connection to the struggles of practitioners still facing persecution. Support networks were established to assist those seeking asylum, while events like candlelight vigils and marches were organized to draw attention to the plight of those who could not practice freely. Through their efforts, these communities became a lifeline for the Falun Gong movement, ensuring its survival and growth beyond its origins.

THE ROLE OF WESTERN ADVOCACY

Western advocacy has been instrumental in amplifying the voices of Falun Gong practitioners and shining a light on their persecution in China. Lawmakers, human rights organizations, and individual activists have played crucial roles in bringing the movement's struggles to global attention. Their efforts have helped to counter disinformation, challenge abuses, and provide a platform for practitioners to share their stories.

Politicians in countries such as the United States, Canada, and the European Union have taken a strong stance against the persecution of Falun Gong. Resolutions condemning the Chinese government's actions have been passed in legislative bodies, and public officials have spoken out in defense of the practice. These statements often come at a diplomatic cost, reflecting the gravity of the issue and the courage of those willing to confront it.

Human rights organizations have also been vital allies. Groups like Amnesty International and Human Rights Watch have documented abuses against Falun Gong practitioners, compiling evidence of arbitrary detention, torture, and forced labor. These reports serve as a foundation for advocacy efforts, providing credible, detailed accounts that challenge the Chinese government's narrative.

Western media has provided another avenue for advocacy. Investigative journalism has uncovered stories of persecution, organ harvesting, and grassroots resistance, exposing these issues to audiences that might otherwise remain unaware. Coverage in prominent outlets has helped to legitimize the movement's concerns, creating pressure on governments and institutions to take action.

Public demonstrations organized by Falun Gong practitioners in the West often include partnerships with local advocacy groups. These collaborations highlight shared values and create a broader coalition of voices calling for justice. The visibility of these events, from candlelight vigils to art exhibitions, helps to humanize the struggle and foster empathy among onlookers.

Advocacy in the West has not been without challenges, as it often faces opposition from Chinese government officials and their allies. However, the persistence of these efforts underscores their importance. For many practitioners, Western advocacy represents a beacon of hope—a reminder that their voices, while suppressed in China, can still resonate loudly on the global stage.

BUILDING INTERNATIONAL AWARENESS

Raising international awareness of Falun Gong's principles and the persecution it faces has been a central focus of the diaspora. Practitioners have developed innovative strategies to engage the global public, using everything from cultural performances to grassroots campaigns. These efforts have transformed Falun Gong from a misunderstood practice into a symbol of resilience and human rights advocacy.

One of the most visible methods has been through public demonstrations. Practitioners often gather in high-traffic areas, performing Falun Gong exercises or holding banners with messages about the persecution. These peaceful demonstrations not only introduce passersby to the practice but also provoke curiosity, sparking conversations that can lead to deeper understanding.

Art and culture have also played a significant role in spreading awareness. Performances like Shen Yun, a touring dance and music company founded by Falun Gong practitioners, showcase traditional Chinese culture while highlighting the spiritual essence of the practice. These performances have reached audiences worldwide, combining entertainment with education about Falun Gong's values and the challenges it faces.

Practitioners have harnessed digital tools to expand their reach, creating websites, social media campaigns, and video content. Platforms like YouTube and Twitter have become vital spaces for sharing testimonials, documenting protests, and exposing human rights violations. By leveraging the internet, practitioners can bypass traditional barriers and connect directly with global audiences.

Awareness campaigns often include petitions and letter-writing drives aimed at influencing policymakers. These efforts encourage individuals to take action, whether by contacting their representatives or supporting initiatives that protect freedom of belief. The personal nature of these campaigns makes them highly effective, as they inspire a sense of individual responsibility and connection to the cause.

The success of these awareness efforts is evident in the growing recognition of Falun Gong worldwide. From local communities to international forums, the practice has gained a platform to share its story, ensuring that its message reaches those who might otherwise remain uninformed. For practitioners, building awareness is not just about spreading the practice but about fostering understanding, empathy, and action on a global scale.

THE ESTABLISHMENT OF MEDIA PLATFORMS

Falun Gong practitioners have created media platforms to counter disinformation, share their stories, and advocate for human rights. These outlets have become powerful tools for amplifying the movement's voice and challenging narratives that distort its principles or downplay its persecution. By creating their own media, practitioners have ensured that their perspectives are represented accurately and compellingly.

One of the most prominent examples is *The Epoch Times*, a global newspaper and digital platform founded by Falun Gong practitioners. Initially launched to document the suppression of Falun Gong in China, the publication has since expanded to cover a wide range of topics, including politics, culture, and human rights. Its investigative reporting has brought attention to issues like organ harvesting, offering evidence and analysis that mainstream outlets often overlook.

Other media initiatives include New Tang Dynasty (NTD) Television, which provides news, cultural programming, and documentaries. NTD has become a key outlet for sharing stories about Falun Gong while promoting traditional Chinese culture. Its broadcasts reach millions of viewers worldwide, offering an alternative perspective to state-controlled narratives.

Digital platforms like YouTube channels and social media accounts have allowed practitioners to reach younger audiences and adapt to changing media consumption habits. Short videos, live-streamed events, and interactive content have made Falun Gong's message accessible to a generation accustomed to consuming information in bite-sized formats.

These media platforms also serve as a way to connect practitioners globally. Newsletters, forums, and online communities facilitate communication and collaboration, allowing practitioners to share resources and strategies. This digital infrastructure has been particularly important in maintaining cohesion and morale among diaspora communities.

Through these platforms, Falun Gong practitioners have reclaimed control over their narrative. By sharing their stories in their own words, they have countered propaganda and misinformation while shining a light on broader issues of freedom and human rights. These media efforts have become a cornerstone of the diaspora's advocacy, ensuring that the practice's message continues to resonate around the world.

BRIDGING CULTURAL GAPS IN PRACTICE

As Falun Gong has spread globally, bridging cultural gaps has become a key part of its adaptation. Rooted in traditional Chinese spirituality, the practice faces the challenge of resonating with diverse cultural contexts while maintaining its authenticity. Practitioners have approached this task with creativity and dedication, finding ways to present Falun Gong's principles in ways that transcend cultural boundaries.

Language has been a significant hurdle, but one that practitioners have tackled with determination. Core texts like

Zhuan Falun have been translated into dozens of languages, ensuring accessibility to non-Chinese speakers. These translations go beyond simple linguistic conversion, incorporating cultural nuances to make the teachings relatable without altering their meaning. Practitioners often collaborate on these efforts, combining linguistic expertise with a deep understanding of the text.

Workshops and open practice sessions have also helped bridge cultural divides. Practitioners host these events in local communities, creating opportunities for people unfamiliar with Falun Gong to experience it firsthand. These sessions often include introductions to the exercises, explanations of the principles, and discussions about the practice's history. By engaging directly with new audiences, practitioners create a welcoming environment that fosters understanding.

Practitioners have also incorporated elements of local culture into their outreach efforts. For example, in Western countries, Falun Gong events often feature elements of Western art, music, or public speaking styles to make the practice more approachable. These adaptations are done thoughtfully, ensuring that they complement rather than dilute the practice's core principles.

Community engagement has been another key strategy. Practitioners participate in local festivals, collaborate with other spiritual groups, and contribute to humanitarian efforts, showcasing Falun Gong as a practice that aligns with universal values. These actions demonstrate the practice's relevance to broader societal goals, helping to dispel misconceptions and foster acceptance.

By bridging cultural gaps, Falun Gong has evolved into a global practice while remaining true to its roots. Practitioners have shown that spirituality is not confined by geography or tradition but can flourish in diverse contexts when approached with openness and respect. This adaptability has been central to Falun Gong's growth and its ability to resonate with people from all walks of life.

COLLABORATION WITH GLOBAL HUMAN RIGHTS GROUPS

The persecution of Falun Gong practitioners in China has drawn significant attention from human rights organizations worldwide. Collaboration with these groups has become a cornerstone of the diaspora's efforts to advocate for freedom of belief and expose abuses. These partnerships amplify the voices of practitioners while contributing to the broader fight for human rights.

Organizations like Amnesty International, Human Rights Watch, and Freedom House have played a critical role in documenting the persecution of Falun Gong. Their reports provide detailed accounts of arbitrary detentions, torture, and other abuses, serving as essential resources for advocacy and awareness campaigns. Practitioners often contribute to these reports, sharing firsthand testimonies that bring the issue to life.

Legal advocacy has also been a key area of collaboration. Practitioners and human rights lawyers have filed lawsuits against Chinese officials accused of orchestrating the persecution. These cases, brought in jurisdictions with universal human rights laws, aim to hold perpetrators accountable and create legal precedents that deter future abuses. Human rights groups often provide support for these efforts, offering expertise and resources.

Collaborative campaigns have also focused on specific issues, such as allegations of forced organ harvesting. Practitioners and human rights organizations have worked together to investigate and expose these practices, organizing hearings, conferences, and public events to raise awareness. These efforts have led to policy changes in some countries, including restrictions on medical tourism to China.

Educational initiatives are another area of partnership. Practitioners and human rights groups frequently collaborate on exhibitions, panel discussions, and media campaigns that highlight the persecution of Falun Gong alongside broader human rights issues. These events create a platform for dialogue, connecting practitioners' struggles to the universal fight for dignity and freedom.

Through these collaborations, Falun Gong practitioners have become an integral part of the global human rights movement. Their experiences and resilience serve as a powerful reminder of the importance of defending freedom of belief, inspiring action and solidarity from people around the world. These partnerships not only amplify their message but also contribute to a larger effort to promote justice and accountability.

THE FUTURE OF FALUN GONG OUTSIDE CHINA

The future of Falun Gong outside China is being shaped by its adaptability, resilience, and global reach. As the practice continues to grow and evolve, practitioners are finding new ways to preserve its essence while addressing the challenges and opportunities of a changing world. These efforts ensure that Falun Gong remains relevant and accessible to future generations.

One area of focus is intergenerational transmission. As many early practitioners age, they are working to pass the practice on to younger generations. This involves not only teaching the exercises and principles but also fostering a deep understanding of Falun Gong's history and values. Youth-focused initiatives, such as workshops and online communities, are helping to engage younger audiences and ensure the practice's continuity.

Technological advancements are also shaping the practice's future. Digital platforms provide new opportunities for outreach, education, and community building. Practitioners are leveraging tools like virtual reality, social media, and apps to create interactive experiences that introduce Falun Gong to a tech-savvy audience. These innovations make the practice more accessible while preserving its core principles.

Cultural integration will remain an important aspect of Falun Gong's evolution. As the practice continues to spread globally, practitioners will need to navigate the balance between adaptation and authenticity. This requires thoughtful engagement with local traditions and customs, ensuring that Falun Gong's message resonates without losing its distinct identity.

The ongoing advocacy for freedom of belief and human rights will also shape Falun Gong's future. The persecution of practitioners in China remains a central issue, driving efforts to raise awareness and support those affected. These advocacy efforts will continue to influence how Falun Gong is perceived and practiced worldwide.

The future of Falun Gong lies in its ability to inspire individuals and communities with its principles of truthfulness, compassion, and forbearance. As practitioners carry the practice forward, they do so with a commitment to its values and a vision of a world where freedom of belief is respected and celebrated. This enduring dedication ensures that Falun Gong will remain a vibrant and meaningful part of the global spiritual landscape.

CONTROVERSIES AND CRITICISMS

ALLEGATIONS AGAINST THE PRACTICE

Falun Gong has faced its share of allegations, ranging from accusations of being a cult to claims that its teachings promote pseudoscience or isolationism. These allegations often come from critics who are skeptical of its rapid growth, its spiritual teachings, or its political implications. While practitioners view Falun Gong as a peaceful and transformative practice, its detractors paint a more contentious picture.

One of the most common allegations is that Falun Gong is a cult. Critics point to its hierarchical structure, with Li Hongzhi at the center, and the devotion many practitioners have for his teachings. They argue that this level of reverence could lead to blind obedience or dependency. Practitioners counter this claim by emphasizing the absence of formal membership, tithing, or centralized control, features often associated with cults.

Another frequent criticism is that Falun Gong promotes anti-scientific views. Detractors cite passages in *Zhuan Falun* where Li discusses phenomena like extraterrestrial life or the effects of karma on health. These ideas are often dismissed as fringe or fantastical. Practitioners, however, argue that these discussions are philosophical in nature and should not be judged by conventional scientific standards.

Some critics allege that Falun Gong encourages social isolation, claiming that practitioners are discouraged from engaging with non-practicing friends and family. This criticism is particularly sensitive, as practitioners insist that the principles of truthfulness, compassion, and forbearance foster stronger relationships, not estrangement. They argue that any perceived isolation stems from misunderstandings or external pressures, such as persecution.

Finally, there are allegations tied to Falun Gong's political activities, particularly its resistance to the Chinese government. Critics claim that the practice has become overly politicized, straying from its spiritual roots. Practitioners maintain that their activism is a response to persecution rather than a political agenda, and they view advocacy as a natural extension of their commitment to truth and justice.

CHALLENGES OF VERIFYING CLAIMS

One of the most significant challenges in understanding Falun Gong lies in verifying the claims made by both its proponents and critics. The practice exists at the intersection of spirituality, politics, and human rights, making it a subject of intense debate and conflicting narratives. Verifying these claims requires navigating a minefield of bias, propaganda, and limited access to reliable data.

In China, the suppression of Falun Gong has created an environment where independent verification is nearly impossible. State-controlled media frequently publishes disinformation about the practice, while practitioners face severe penalties for speaking out. This dynamic makes it difficult for outsiders to determine the accuracy of allegations, such as claims of harm caused by the practice or the extent of the persecution.

Outside of China, the situation is complicated by the polarizing nature of the discourse. Practitioners often present personal testimonies of transformation or resilience, while critics highlight selective anecdotes or controversial passages from *Zhuan Falun*. Both perspectives are deeply influenced by personal experiences and biases, making it hard to separate objective facts from subjective interpretations.

Academic studies on Falun Gong are scarce and often inconclusive. Some researchers focus on its health benefits or spiritual teachings, while others examine its role in Chinese politics and society. The lack of comprehensive, peer-reviewed studies leaves gaps in the understanding of the practice, further fueling the controversy.

Verification is also hindered by the sheer diversity of Falun Gong practitioners and their experiences. While some describe profound physical and emotional healing, others report challenges or even disillusionment. This variation reflects the highly personal nature of spiritual practice, complicating efforts to generalize about its effects or implications.

The challenge of verifying claims underscores the importance of critical thinking and open dialogue. Rather than taking any single perspective at face value, observers are encouraged to consider multiple sources and perspectives. This approach, while time-consuming, offers the best chance of understanding Falun Gong in all its complexity.

SEPARATING FACT FROM FICTION

When it comes to Falun Gong, separating fact from fiction can feel like navigating a hall of mirrors. Both critics and supporters offer passionate accounts, but their stories often diverge dramatically. This disconnect creates a confusing narrative where truth, misrepresentation, and outright fabrication coexist, challenging even the most discerning observers.

One area where fiction often creeps in is the characterization of Li Hongzhi. Critics sometimes portray him as an authoritarian figure who demands unwavering loyalty, while practitioners describe him as a humble teacher who encourages self-reflection and personal responsibility. The reality likely lies somewhere in between, shaped by individual interpretations and cultural perspectives.

Media coverage of Falun Gong often amplifies misunderstandings. Sensational headlines focus on controversial aspects, such as allegations of anti-scientific teachings or extreme devotion. These portrayals can obscure the more mundane reality of daily practice, which for most practitioners involves meditative exercises and efforts to improve moral character.

Propaganda from the Chinese government adds another layer of distortion. Official narratives frequently depict Falun Gong as a dangerous cult, citing incidents that are difficult to verify independently. Practitioners argue that these accounts are fabricated to justify persecution, further muddying the waters for those trying to understand the practice objectively.

Efforts to separate fact from fiction are also complicated by the diversity of Falun Gong's global presence. In some countries, practitioners focus primarily on spiritual growth, while in others, advocacy against persecution takes center stage. These differences reflect the adaptability of the practice but can also create confusion about its core identity and goals.

Ultimately, separating fact from fiction requires patience and a willingness to engage with multiple perspectives. By approaching the topic with curiosity rather than preconceived notions, observers can begin to untangle the complex web of narratives surrounding Falun Gong, gaining a clearer understanding of its practices and controversies.

INTERNAL CONFLICTS AMONG PRACTITIONERS

Like any global movement, Falun Gong has experienced its share of internal conflicts. These disagreements often arise from differing interpretations of the teachings, varying approaches to activism, or cultural and personal differences among practitioners. While the practice emphasizes harmony and self-cultivation, the reality of human dynamics ensures that conflicts occasionally emerge.

One source of tension is the interpretation of *Zhuan Falun*. While the text serves as the foundation for the practice, its abstract and philosophical nature leaves room for diverse understandings. Practitioners sometimes disagree on how to apply its principles in specific situations, leading to debates about the "correct" way to practice. These disagreements, while usually respectful, can create friction within local communities.

Activism has also been a point of contention. Some practitioners prioritize advocacy against persecution, organizing protests, distributing leaflets, or engaging with the media. Others feel that such activities detract from the spiritual essence of the practice, arguing that true change comes from internal cultivation rather than external efforts. Balancing these perspectives is an ongoing challenge.

Cultural differences further complicate internal dynamics. As Falun Gong has spread globally, practitioners from diverse backgrounds have brought their own customs and expectations to the practice. While this diversity enriches the movement, it can also lead to misunderstandings or clashes over priorities and approaches.

Leadership within local communities is another area where conflicts sometimes arise. Although Falun Gong lacks a formal hierarchy, informal leaders often emerge to coordinate activities or provide guidance. Disagreements about leadership styles or decisions can create tension, particularly in communities where strong personalities are involved.

Despite these conflicts, practitioners often describe them as opportunities for growth. The principles of truthfulness, compassion, and forbearance serve as guiding lights, encouraging individuals to resolve disagreements with patience and understanding. In this way, internal conflicts become a microcosm of the broader challenges of self-cultivation, reflecting the complexities of human relationships and the resilience of the practice.

ADDRESSING SKEPTICISM AND OPPOSITION

Falun Gong practitioners have faced skepticism and opposition from various sources, ranging from curious onlookers to vocal critics. Addressing these challenges requires a mix of patience, openness, and clear communication. Practitioners often view such encounters as opportunities to clarify misconceptions and share their experiences, even when the conversation takes an uncomfortable turn.

One common point of skepticism revolves around the perceived esotericism of Falun Gong's teachings. Critics may question concepts like the Law Wheel (*Falun*) or the spiritual dimensions described in *Zhuan Falun*. Practitioners respond by emphasizing that these ideas are meant to be understood experientially rather than intellectually. They often draw parallels to similar concepts in other spiritual traditions, hoping to foster a sense of relatability.

Opposition can also stem from the practice's visibility in public spaces. Demonstrations, exercise sessions, and advocacy campaigns sometimes provoke criticism from those who view them as intrusive or disruptive. Practitioners typically counter this by explaining the purpose of their activities, whether it's raising awareness of persecution or simply sharing the practice with others. Many stress that their actions are peaceful and inclusive, aiming to create understanding rather than conflict.

Critics often question Falun Gong's relationship with science and medicine, particularly in relation to claims of healing through spiritual practice. Practitioners acknowledge that Falun Gong is not a substitute for medical care but argue that the practice's emphasis on morality and mindfulness has genuine benefits for mental and physical health. They frequently cite personal testimonials or point to studies on the effects of meditation and qigong as evidence.

Skepticism about Falun Gong's political activities also arises, especially regarding its advocacy against the Chinese government. Critics sometimes accuse the practice of being overly confrontational or politicized. Practitioners respond by framing their actions as a defense of human rights rather than political opposition. They emphasize that their activism is a direct response to persecution, grounded in the practice's core principles of truthfulness and compassion.

Addressing skepticism is not always easy, but practitioners often see it as a necessary part of their journey. By engaging with critics thoughtfully and respectfully, they hope to foster understanding and bridge divides. For many, these conversations are not just about defending Falun Gong but about living its principles in real-time, demonstrating the practice's values through their actions.

HOW PRACTITIONERS RESPOND TO CRITICISMS

Falun Gong practitioners have developed a variety of strategies for responding to criticisms, ranging from public advocacy to private reflection. Their approach is deeply influenced by the practice's principles, emphasizing patience, empathy, and a commitment to truth. Whether addressing misunderstandings or outright hostility, practitioners strive to turn criticism into an opportunity for dialogue and growth.

Publicly, practitioners often respond to criticisms through informational campaigns. They distribute leaflets, organize forums, and host Q&A sessions to explain the practice and address common misconceptions. These efforts are designed to be educational rather than confrontational, focusing on clarifying misunderstandings rather than debating detractors. Practitioners often cite their personal experiences to make their responses relatable and authentic.

Digital platforms have also become a key tool for addressing criticisms. Practitioners use websites, blogs, and social media to share detailed explanations of Falun Gong's teachings and history. These platforms allow them to reach a wide audience and respond to specific concerns in a thoughtful and comprehensive manner. Videos, infographics, and testimonials add depth and accessibility to their messaging.

When faced with direct criticism, practitioners are encouraged to respond with compassion and understanding. They view such interactions as a chance to embody the practice's principles, even when the conversation becomes heated or dismissive. Many describe these moments as tests of their forbearance, challenging them to remain calm and respectful while standing firm in their beliefs.

Internal reflection also plays a role in responding to criticisms. Practitioners often use criticism as an opportunity to examine their own actions and attitudes, asking whether they could have communicated more effectively or approached the situation differently. This process of self-assessment aligns with the practice's emphasis on self-cultivation, turning external challenges into opportunities for personal growth.

Ultimately, practitioners see their responses to criticism as a reflection of Falun Gong itself. By approaching these situations with sincerity and humility, they aim to demonstrate the practice's values in action. For many, this is the most powerful way to address criticisms, offering a living example of what Falun Gong stands for.

THE ROLE OF OBJECTIVITY IN UNDERSTANDING FALUN GONG

Objectivity plays a critical role in understanding Falun Gong, particularly given the polarizing nature of the narratives surrounding it. With passionate advocates on one side and vocal critics on the other, observers often find themselves navigating a complex and sometimes contradictory landscape. Taking an objective approach is essential for separating fact from opinion and gaining a balanced perspective.

One challenge to objectivity is the highly charged political context in which Falun Gong exists. The Chinese government's campaign against the practice has generated a wealth of propaganda, much of which is designed to discredit Falun Gong and justify its suppression. At the same time, practitioners' efforts to counter these narratives can sometimes lead to equally one-sided portrayals. Observers must sift through these competing accounts with care.

Media coverage also complicates efforts to maintain objectivity. Sensational headlines and oversimplified narratives often dominate discussions of Falun Gong, obscuring its complexities. Readers are encouraged to go beyond surface-level reporting and seek out primary sources, such as *Zhuan Falun*, practitioner testimonials, and independent investigations. This approach allows for a more nuanced understanding of the practice and its context.

Academic research provides another avenue for objectivity, though it is not without limitations. Studies on Falun Gong range from analyses of its health benefits to examinations of its role in Chinese society. While these studies offer valuable insights, they are often constrained by limited access to data and the difficulty of conducting fieldwork in China. Observers should approach academic findings as one piece of a larger puzzle.

Engaging directly with practitioners can also enhance objectivity. Hearing their stories and asking questions allows for a deeper understanding of their motivations and experiences. This firsthand perspective helps to humanize the practice and challenge preconceived notions, creating a more balanced view.

Objectivity requires an open mind and a willingness to engage with complexity. By approaching Falun Gong with curiosity and critical thinking, observers can move beyond polarized narratives and appreciate the practice for what it is: a multifaceted movement shaped by spirituality, resilience, and a commitment to its principles. This balanced perspective is not just valuable for understanding Falun Gong but for fostering dialogue and mutual respect in a world often divided by differing beliefs.

THE HEALTH BENEFITS OF FALUN GONG

SCIENTIFIC STUDIES ON MEDITATION AND HEALTH

The relationship between meditation and health has fascinated scientists for decades, and Falun Gong's practices have naturally drawn attention within this growing field of research. Studies on meditation reveal numerous physiological and psychological benefits, many of which align with the experiences reported by practitioners. While specific research on Falun Gong remains limited due to political challenges, the broader science of meditation provides valuable insights.

Research consistently shows that meditation reduces stress by calming the autonomic nervous system. Practices like those in Falun Gong activate the parasympathetic response, lowering heart rates, reducing blood pressure, and mitigating cortisol levels. For practitioners, this means an improved sense of relaxation and focus, which they often describe as "lighter" or "clearer" after exercise sessions.

Brain imaging studies add another layer to the understanding of meditation's effects. Techniques like fMRI reveal that meditation enhances activity in areas associated with emotional regulation and self-awareness. Practitioners of Falun Gong frequently report increased emotional stability, and scientific findings suggest this could stem from these neural changes. Though these studies don't isolate Falun Gong specifically, they support the broader claim that consistent meditation rewires the brain for resilience.

The immune system also seems to benefit from meditation. Several studies show that meditative practices enhance the activity of natural killer cells and antibodies, critical components in fighting infections. Falun Gong practitioners often credit their exercises and meditative focus for helping them recover from illnesses or avoid seasonal ailments altogether. While anecdotal, these reports mirror findings in clinical research on immune health.

One intriguing area of research involves the effect of meditation on gene expression. Emerging studies suggest that consistent meditation can suppress genes associated with inflammation and activate those linked to stress resistance. Practitioners' accounts of improved physical health and vitality could very well tie into these molecular changes, making Falun Gong's exercises more than just a mental reprieve—they might also alter the body at a cellular level.

JEANNIE LEE

TESTIMONIALS FROM PRACTITIONERS

Practitioners of Falun Gong often describe profound transformations in their physical and mental health, recounting stories that are as compelling as they are diverse. While personal accounts may not meet the rigor of clinical trials, they offer a glimpse into how the practice impacts individual lives. These testimonials, shared in community meetings, media outlets, and even casual conversations, form a powerful narrative of healing and resilience.

One common theme among practitioners' stories is relief from chronic pain. Many describe years of suffering from conditions like arthritis, migraines, or back problems before discovering Falun Gong. Through consistent practice of the exercises and adherence to its principles, they report significant reductions in pain, increased mobility, and improved quality of life. These transformations are often attributed to the unblocking of energy pathways, a concept central to Falun Gong.

Mental health improvements are another frequent subject of testimonials. Practitioners speak of finding peace after struggling with anxiety, depression, or trauma. For many, the practice provides a structured way to process emotions, cultivate patience, and approach life with clarity. The combination of physical exercises and spiritual teachings seems to create a holistic approach that addresses both symptoms and underlying causes.

Several practitioners recount experiences of overcoming serious illnesses, from autoimmune disorders to cancer. While such claims remain controversial, they underscore the belief that Falun Gong's emphasis on self-cultivation and mindfulness can unlock the body's natural healing potential. These stories often inspire others to explore the practice, drawn by the hope of similar outcomes.

Testimonials also highlight the community aspect of Falun Gong. Practicing in groups offers both encouragement and accountability, creating a support network that bolsters individual efforts. For many, the shared experience of healing becomes a cornerstone of their journey, reinforcing their commitment to the practice and its principles.

THE ROLE OF MIND-BODY CONNECTION

At the heart of Falun Gong's health benefits lies the mind-body connection, a concept that bridges the physical and the spiritual. The practice emphasizes that the mind's state directly influences the body, a principle supported by both ancient wisdom and modern science. For practitioners, this connection manifests in tangible ways, linking their thoughts, emotions, and physical health.

The exercises in Falun Gong are designed to harmonize the body and mind, fostering a state of balance that promotes healing. The slow, deliberate movements encourage practitioners to focus on their breath, posture, and energy flow, creating a meditative state that calms the mind. This mindfulness has ripple effects, reducing stress and improving physiological functions like digestion and circulation.

The practice's emphasis on truthfulness, compassion, and forbearance further strengthens the mind-body link. Practitioners often describe how adopting these principles transforms their emotional landscape, reducing anger, resentment, and anxiety. These emotional shifts, in turn, alleviate physical symptoms like tension headaches or digestive issues, illustrating the interconnected nature of well-being.

Scientific research supports the idea that positive mental states can enhance physical health. Studies show that mindfulness practices like Falun Gong improve heart rate variability, a key indicator of stress resilience. Practitioners often notice this in their day-to-day lives, describing a greater ability to remain calm in challenging situations, which contributes to better long-term health.

For many practitioners, the mind-body connection is not just a theory but a lived experience. They often recount moments when emotional breakthroughs coincided with physical healing, reinforcing their belief in the practice's power. This holistic approach offers a compelling alternative to treatments that focus solely on the body, emphasizing the importance of nurturing both mental and physical health.

STRENGTHENING MENTAL RESILIENCE

Mental resilience is one of the most celebrated benefits of Falun Gong, with practitioners frequently describing a newfound ability to handle life's challenges with grace and strength. This resilience is cultivated through a combination of meditative exercises, spiritual teachings, and personal reflection, all of which contribute to a more balanced and grounded state of mind.

The meditative aspects of Falun Gong help practitioners develop focus and clarity. By engaging in exercises that require mindful attention to movement and breath, they learn to quiet mental chatter and approach life with a clearer perspective. This skill translates to daily situations, enabling practitioners to manage stress and remain composed under pressure.

Falun Gong's teachings encourage practitioners to view challenges as opportunities for growth rather than obstacles. This mindset shift fosters resilience as practitioners approach difficulties with patience and a willingness to learn. For example, conflicts at work or home become chances to practice forbearance, a principle that strengthens their emotional endurance.

The community aspect of Falun Gong also contributes to mental resilience. Practicing in groups creates a sense of solidarity and support, reducing feelings of isolation. Sharing experiences and insights with others reinforces the practice's teachings and provides encouragement during difficult times. This collective strength becomes a source of motivation and stability.

Many practitioners credit Falun Gong with helping them develop a deeper sense of purpose and self-worth. By aligning their actions with the principles of truthfulness, compassion, and forbearance, they find a moral compass that guides them through life's uncertainties. This sense of alignment creates a foundation of confidence and inner peace, further bolstering their resilience.

Mental resilience cultivated through Falun Gong often extends beyond the individual. Practitioners report that their improved emotional stability benefits their relationships, workplaces, and communities. This ripple effect underscores the practice's holistic nature, showing how personal transformation can contribute to broader harmony and well-being.

ADDRESSING CHRONIC ILLNESSES THROUGH PRACTICE

For many practitioners, Falun Gong offers hope in addressing chronic illnesses that conventional medicine struggles to resolve. While the practice is not presented as a cure-all, its combination of meditative exercises, mindfulness, and moral principles often leads to reports of improved health. These stories, though anecdotal, illustrate the potential of an integrative approach to managing long-term conditions.

Practitioners with conditions such as arthritis, fibromyalgia, and chronic fatigue syndrome frequently report reductions in pain and increased mobility after adopting Falun Gong. The slow, flowing movements of the exercises appear to relieve tension and improve circulation, providing physical relief. Additionally, the practice's meditative aspects help manage the psychological toll of chronic pain, fostering a sense of control and hope.

Respiratory and cardiovascular health are also areas where practitioners have noted benefits. Those with asthma or high blood pressure often describe improvements in their symptoms, attributing them to the calming effects of meditation and the focus on breath control during exercises. These changes align with broader research on the physiological effects of mindfulness and slow, rhythmic movements.

For individuals with autoimmune conditions, the practice's emphasis on reducing stress and fostering emotional balance seems to play a critical role. Practitioners often describe how adopting Falun Gong's principles helps them release negative emotions and cultivate a more positive mindset. This shift can reduce stress-related inflammation, potentially alleviating symptoms associated with autoimmune disorders.

Cancer patients and survivors have shared some of the most remarkable testimonials. While Falun Gong is not a replacement for medical treatment, many credit the practice with aiding their recovery and enhancing their quality of life. They often cite the practice's focus on moral improvement and energy balance as key factors in their healing journey. These stories, while not scientifically verified, highlight the profound impact the practice can have on individuals' physical and emotional well-being.

CHALLENGES IN ESTABLISHING EVIDENCE

Despite numerous testimonials and anecdotal accounts, establishing scientific evidence for Falun Gong's health benefits remains a significant challenge. The political context surrounding the practice complicates research efforts, particularly in China, where access to practitioners and unbiased data is severely limited. This lack of robust studies leaves a gap in understanding the full extent of the practice's effects.

One challenge lies in the nature of the practice itself. Falun Gong emphasizes self-cultivation and personal responsibility, making it difficult to standardize for clinical trials. Unlike pharmaceutical interventions, which can be uniformly administered, Falun Gong's benefits depend on individual engagement with its exercises and teachings. This variability complicates efforts to measure its efficacy in controlled settings.

Another issue is the reliance on self-reported outcomes. While testimonials provide valuable insights, they lack the rigor of randomized controlled trials or peer-reviewed research. Skeptics argue that the placebo effect or natural variations in health may explain some of the reported benefits. Practitioners, however, maintain that their experiences are genuine and transformative, even if they cannot always be quantified.

Political interference has also hindered research on Falun Gong. In China, where the practice originated, government suppression has created an environment of fear and censorship. Researchers risk backlash for studying the practice, and practitioners may be reluctant to participate in studies. This dynamic limits access to a critical population, skewing the available data.

Outside of China, interest in studying Falun Gong is growing, but funding and institutional support remain limited. Most research on related practices, such as qigong and mindfulness, is conducted in broader contexts, leaving questions about how Falun Gong's specific principles and exercises contribute to its effects. Bridging this gap requires dedicated resources and a commitment to objective inquiry.

FALUN GONG AS A COMPLEMENTARY PRACTICE

Falun Gong is often viewed by practitioners as a complementary practice that enhances, rather than replaces, conventional healthcare. Its focus on holistic well-being aligns with the growing interest in integrative medicine, which combines traditional treatments with alternative approaches. This perspective allows individuals to benefit from both worlds, using Falun Gong to support their physical and emotional health while seeking medical care when needed.

One way Falun Gong complements conventional medicine is by addressing the emotional and psychological aspects of health. Many chronic illnesses, such as diabetes or heart disease, are exacerbated by stress and poor mental health. Practicing Falun Gong helps individuals manage stress and cultivate a more positive outlook, creating a supportive environment for healing.

The practice's emphasis on moral principles also plays a role in its complementary nature. By encouraging truthfulness, compassion, and forbearance, Falun Gong fosters habits that align with healthy living. Practitioners often report making better lifestyle choices, such as eating more mindfully, exercising regularly, or quitting harmful habits, as a result of their practice.

Falun Gong's exercises provide gentle physical activity that can be tailored to individual needs. For people recovering from surgery or managing mobility issues, the low-impact movements offer a safe way to maintain physical health. Practitioners often describe these exercises as restorative, providing energy and flexibility without strain.

Perhaps most importantly, Falun Gong empowers individuals to take an active role in their health. By combining meditative exercises with a focus on self-improvement, it encourages a mindset of responsibility and agency. This proactive approach complements medical treatments, fostering a sense of partnership between practitioners and their healthcare providers.

For many, Falun Gong represents a bridge between the spiritual and the physical, offering tools that enhance their overall well-being. Whether used alongside medication, therapy, or other interventions, the practice provides a framework for cultivating balance and resilience in the face of life's challenges. Its adaptability and holistic focus make it a valuable addition to the landscape of complementary health practices.

FALUN GONG IN POPULAR CULTURE

DEPICTIONS IN MEDIA AND LITERATURE

Falun Gong's portrayal in media and literature has been as diverse as its global impact, with narratives ranging from sympathetic to sensationalized. Its intersection with popular culture offers a window into how society grapples with complex topics like spirituality, human rights, and political resistance. The way Falun Gong is depicted often reflects broader cultural, social, or political agendas.

In literature, Falun Gong has appeared as both subject and subtext, often framed within larger narratives about modern China. Fictionalized accounts sometimes present practitioners as stoic heroes resisting oppression, while others use the practice as a backdrop for exploring themes of faith and personal transformation. These portrayals vary widely in accuracy, often shaped by the author's perspective and their understanding—or misunderstanding—of the practice.

News media coverage has been a battleground for competing narratives. State-run Chinese outlets portray Falun Gong in a consistently negative light, accusing it of everything from destabilizing society to promoting dangerous ideologies. Outside China, media coverage often emphasizes the human rights violations practitioners face, presenting the practice as a symbol of resilience. These polarized portrayals leave readers navigating a maze of conflicting stories.

Television and film have occasionally touched on Falun Gong, though often in passing. Western productions, particularly documentaries, focus on the practice's human rights struggles. Meanwhile, Chinese dramas and propaganda films depict practitioners as deluded or even dangerous, perpetuating the government's anti-Falun Gong narrative. These depictions are rarely neutral, reflecting the contentious context in which they are created.

Social media has added a new dimension to Falun Gong's presence in popular culture. Platforms like Twitter, Instagram, and YouTube are used by practitioners to share their stories and by critics to voice opposition. This digital landscape provides a more direct and personal lens into Falun Gong's impact, bypassing traditional gatekeepers and giving audiences a chance to hear from practitioners themselves.

ARTISTIC EXPRESSIONS INSPIRED BY FALUN GONG

Art has become a powerful medium for expressing the principles and experiences of Falun Gong, blending creativity with advocacy. From traditional paintings to modern installations, practitioners have used their talents to share the beauty of their practice and highlight the challenges they face. These works often reflect the themes of truthfulness, compassion, and forbearance, resonating with audiences regardless of their familiarity with Falun Gong.

Traditional Chinese painting and calligraphy have been popular forms of expression among practitioners. These artworks often depict serene landscapes, lotus flowers, or scenes of meditation, symbolizing the spiritual aspects of Falun Gong. Others incorporate imagery of the persecution in China, contrasting the tranquility of the practice with the harsh realities practitioners endure. These pieces invite viewers to reflect on the duality of beauty and struggle.

Modern art has also found a place within the Falun Gong community. Sculptures, photography, and mixed-media installations explore the practice's teachings through contemporary aesthetics. Some pieces are deeply personal, capturing moments of resilience or transformation, while others are explicitly political, challenging viewers to confront the human rights abuses associated with the practice.

Performing arts offer another outlet for artistic expression. Practitioners have created dance and theater productions that convey Falun Gong's principles through movement and storytelling. These performances often blend traditional Chinese techniques with modern choreography, creating a unique fusion that appeals to diverse audiences.

Art exhibitions featuring works by practitioners have become a staple of Falun Gong's cultural outreach. These events, held in galleries and community centers worldwide, serve as both artistic showcases and advocacy platforms. Visitors are often moved by the emotional depth and technical skill of the pieces, gaining a deeper appreciation for the practice and its impact.

Through their art, practitioners bridge the gap between personal experience and public awareness. Their creations offer a tangible connection to the values and struggles of Falun Gong, inspiring empathy and understanding. In this way, art becomes more than a form of expression—it becomes a tool for connection and change.

DOCUMENTARIES AND ADVOCACY FILMS

The story of Falun Gong has been captured in numerous documentaries and advocacy films, offering an intimate look at the practice and its challenges. These films often blend personal narratives with broader social and political commentary, creating powerful stories that resonate with audiences around the world. For many viewers, these documentaries serve as an introduction to Falun Gong and its struggles.

One of the most striking features of these films is their focus on human rights. Documentaries like *Free China: The Courage to Believe* and *Human Harvest* explore the persecution faced by practitioners, from detention and torture to allegations of forced organ harvesting. These films often rely on firsthand accounts, bringing viewers face-to-face with the realities of life for Falun Gong practitioners in China.

Another common theme is resilience. Filmmakers highlight the strength and determination of practitioners who continue their practice despite immense challenges. Their stories of resistance, whether through peaceful protests or quiet acts of defiance, inspire audiences and challenge perceptions of what it means to stand up for one's beliefs.

The production of these films is often an act of courage in itself. Many filmmakers face significant risks, from censorship to threats, particularly when working within or near China. This adds a layer of urgency and authenticity to their work, as they document a story that might otherwise go untold.

Advocacy films frequently use creative techniques to engage viewers. Animated sequences, dramatic reenactments, and compelling musical scores draw audiences into the narrative, making complex issues accessible and emotionally impactful. These elements help bridge the gap between information and empathy, turning abstract concepts into deeply personal stories.

By sharing the story of Falun Gong through film, these documentaries amplify voices that might otherwise be silenced. They provide a platform for practitioners to share their experiences and for audiences to engage with the practice's principles and struggles. In doing so, they contribute to a growing awareness and understanding of Falun Gong in popular culture.

ROLE OF SHEN YUN IN CULTURAL OUTREACH

Shen Yun Performing Arts has become one of the most recognizable symbols of Falun Gong's cultural outreach. This touring dance and music company showcases traditional Chinese culture while promoting the values of truthfulness, compassion, and forbearance. With its vibrant costumes, intricate choreography, and live orchestras, Shen

Yun has captivated audiences worldwide, creating a cultural phenomenon in its own right.

At the heart of Shen Yun is a celebration of traditional Chinese arts, from classical dance to ancient instruments. Each performance features a series of vignettes, often drawing from historical tales, folklore, or spiritual themes. These stories highlight the richness of Chinese heritage while weaving in elements of Falun Gong's teachings, creating a narrative that bridges the past and present.

Shen Yun's performances are also a form of advocacy, shining a light on the persecution of Falun Gong in China. Through dance and music, the company tells stories of practitioners standing firm in their beliefs despite oppression. These segments are deeply moving, offering a powerful contrast to the show's otherwise uplifting tone. For many audience members, these moments are a poignant introduction to the struggles faced by Falun Gong practitioners.

The production values of Shen Yun are a major draw. From elaborate backdrops that use cutting-edge digital technology to meticulously crafted costumes, every detail is designed to create a visually stunning experience. The company's commitment to excellence has earned it praise from critics and audiences alike, further elevating its cultural impact.

Shen Yun's global reach is another testament to its success. With performances in cities across the Americas, Europe, Asia, and beyond, the company has introduced millions to both traditional Chinese culture and Falun Gong's principles. For practitioners, Shen Yun represents not just an artistic endeavor but a way to share their values and stories with the world.

PUBLIC FIGURES AND FALUN GONG

Over the years, several public figures have spoken about or interacted with Falun Gong, bringing additional attention to the practice. From politicians to artists, these individuals have played a role in shaping the public's perception of Falun Gong and its place in society. Their involvement often reflects broader themes of human rights, spirituality, and cultural exchange.

Some politicians have championed Falun Gong as part of their advocacy for religious freedom and human rights. Members of Congress, parliamentarians, and other officials have passed resolutions or issued statements condemning the persecution of practitioners in China. Their support lends credibility to Falun Gong's cause and places it within the larger context of global human rights efforts.

Artists and performers have also drawn inspiration from Falun Gong. Musicians have composed pieces based on their principles, while visual artists have created works that reflect their themes. These collaborations often bring fresh perspectives to the practice, expanding its reach and appeal.

Celebrities have occasionally voiced support for Falun Gong, particularly in the context of human rights. While their involvement is often limited to statements or appearances, it helps raise awareness among their audiences. These endorsements can spark curiosity and encourage people to learn more about the practice and its challenges.

Academics and intellectuals have contributed to the discourse on Falun Gong through research, lectures, and publications. Their work often provides a more nuanced understanding of the practice, countering stereotypes or misconceptions. By placing Falun Gong within historical, cultural, and philosophical contexts, they enrich the conversation around its significance.

Public figures' engagement with Falun Gong highlights its intersection with broader societal issues. Whether through advocacy, art, or scholarship, their contributions help bring the practice into mainstream consciousness, fostering dialogue and understanding. For practitioners, this support represents both validation and an opportunity to share their stories with new audiences.

CULTURAL CONTRIBUTIONS BY PRACTITIONERS

Falun Gong practitioners have made significant cultural contributions, infusing their principles and experiences into various artistic and intellectual pursuits. These contributions serve as a bridge between the practice and broader society, showcasing the creativity and resilience of practitioners while introducing Falun Gong to new audiences. From literature to performing arts, their work reflects a deep commitment to truthfulness, compassion, and forbearance.

In literature, practitioners have authored memoirs, novels, and poetry that explore their personal journeys and the practice's teachings. Memoirs often recount experiences of transformation or resilience, providing intimate glimpses into the challenges and triumphs of Falun Gong practitioners. Novels inspired by Falun Gong frequently weave its principles into fictional narratives, creating compelling stories that resonate with universal themes of justice, courage, and spiritual growth.

The performing arts are another arena where practitioners shine. Dance troupes, theater productions, and music ensembles led by practitioners bring traditional Chinese art forms to life, often blending them with elements of Falun Gong. These performances celebrate cultural heritage while offering a contemporary perspective on spiritual and moral values. Audiences frequently describe these productions as both entertaining and thought-provoking.

Visual arts, including painting and sculpture, also play a prominent role in practitioners' cultural contributions. Art exhibitions featuring works by Falun Gong practitioners often highlight themes of harmony, resilience, and freedom. Many pieces depict scenes of meditation or the persecution of practitioners, inviting viewers to reflect on the practice's deeper meanings and the struggles faced by its followers.

Academic contributions by practitioners add another layer to their cultural impact. Researchers and educators who practice Falun Gong have integrated its principles into their work, exploring topics ranging from ethics to mindfulness. Their efforts often challenge conventional paradigms, offering fresh perspectives that encourage critical thinking and dialogue.

These cultural contributions not only enrich the arts and sciences but also foster a greater understanding of Falun Gong. They provide a platform for practitioners to share their values and experiences, breaking down barriers and building connections with diverse audiences. For many, these creative endeavors are a way to live out the principles of Falun Gong, turning their talents into tools for inspiration and change.

EVOLVING IMAGE OF FALUN GONG

The image of Falun Gong has evolved significantly since its emergence in the 1990s, shaped by shifting narratives, global advocacy, and cultural engagement. From a relatively obscure qigong practice to a worldwide movement, Falun Gong's journey reflects its adaptability and resilience. Understanding this evolution offers insight into how the practice navigates complex social and political landscapes.

In its early years, Falun Gong was primarily viewed as a health and wellness practice, attracting millions in China with its meditative exercises and moral teachings. Media coverage often highlighted its positive effects on physical and mental health, portraying it as part of a broader qigong revival. This period of recognition and growth set the stage for Falun Gong's rise as a prominent spiritual movement.

The crackdown in 1999 drastically altered Falun Gong's image, particularly within China. State propaganda framed the practice as a threat to social stability, branding it as a dangerous cult. This narrative was aggressively promoted through media campaigns, reshaping public perception and driving a wedge between practitioners and broader society. Outside China, however, these efforts sparked international outrage and positioned Falun Gong as a symbol of resistance against authoritarianism.

Global advocacy and cultural outreach have further shaped Falun Gong's image. Initiatives like Shen Yun and art exhibitions present the practice as a celebration of traditional values and human dignity. These efforts highlight its spiritual and cultural dimensions, countering stereotypes and fostering empathy. For many, Falun Gong has become synonymous with resilience, creativity, and a commitment to truth.

Social media and digital platforms have added new layers to Falun Gong's evolving image. Practitioners use these tools to share their stories and connect with audiences worldwide, bypassing traditional media gatekeepers. These platforms allow for more nuanced and personal portrayals of the practice, helping to demystify its teachings and address misconceptions.

The evolving image of Falun Gong underscores its dynamic nature. It is not just a static set of teachings but a living, adaptive practice shaped by the experiences of its practitioners and the challenges they face. This evolution reflects both the resilience of the movement and the enduring appeal of its principles, ensuring its relevance in an ever-changing world.

THE PATH FORWARD FOR FALUN GONG

ADAPTING TO A CHANGING WORLD

As the world evolves, Falun Gong faces the challenge of staying relevant while maintaining its core principles. The practice emerged in a vastly different time, rooted in traditional Chinese culture but quickly adapting to global contexts. Today, it must navigate the complexities of modern life, from rapid technological advancements to shifting cultural attitudes, all while preserving its essence.

One way Falun Gong has adapted is by embracing diverse cultural interpretations of its teachings. Practitioners from different backgrounds bring unique perspectives to the practice, often enriching its application. This diversity has allowed Falun Gong to resonate across cultures, creating a global network of individuals who see its principles as universal and timeless. However, adapting without losing its identity requires careful balance, ensuring the teachings remain authentic.

Modern lifestyles, with their emphasis on convenience and immediacy, present another challenge. Falun Gong's practices, which require dedication and patience, may seem at odds with a fast-paced world. Practitioners address this by highlighting the practice's accessibility—exercises that can be done anywhere, texts that are freely available, and a structure that allows individuals to practice on their own terms. This flexibility helps bridge the gap between ancient traditions and contemporary needs.

Adapting to a changing world also means addressing new forms of stress and distraction. Digital devices, social media, and constant connectivity often leave individuals feeling overwhelmed. Falun Gong's emphasis on mindfulness and spiritual grounding offers a counterbalance to these pressures. Practitioners find that incorporating the practice into their daily routines provides a sense of clarity and focus, helping them navigate modern challenges.

The practice's ability to adapt while staying true to its principles is a testament to its resilience. Falun Gong's teachings emphasize personal cultivation, which inherently includes the capacity to evolve. By remaining grounded in truthfulness, compassion, and forbearance, practitioners can meet the demands of a changing world without compromising the integrity of their practice.

CHALLENGES FACING FUTURE GENERATIONS

Future generations of Falun Gong practitioners face unique challenges as they inherit the practice in a rapidly transforming world. While the foundational principles of Falun

Gong remain unchanged, the social, political, and cultural landscapes in which it exists are constantly shifting. This creates both opportunities and obstacles for those who will carry the practice forward.

One challenge lies in maintaining interest and engagement among younger generations. Today's youth grow up in an environment saturated with distractions, from social media to video games. Practitioners must find ways to present Falun Gong in a way that appeals to this audience without diluting its teachings. This may involve integrating the practice with digital tools, creating interactive content, or fostering youth-focused communities that provide a sense of belonging.

Education is another key concern. As older practitioners pass on their knowledge, ensuring the accuracy and depth of their teachings becomes paramount. Younger generations must not only learn the exercises but also understand the philosophical and spiritual dimensions of the practice. This requires thoughtful mentorship, accessible resources, and opportunities for deeper engagement with Falun Gong's core texts.

The political climate surrounding Falun Gong adds another layer of complexity. The suppression of the practice in China remains a significant issue, shaping how younger practitioners approach advocacy and activism. They must navigate the delicate balance between preserving their spiritual focus and addressing the human rights violations that affect their community. This requires resilience, creativity, and a strong sense of purpose.

Cultural shifts also pose challenges. As societies become more secular and skeptical of spiritual practices, younger practitioners may encounter criticism or misunderstanding. They must learn to articulate the value of Falun Gong in ways that resonate with contemporary audiences, emphasizing its relevance to modern life while staying true to its roots.

Despite these challenges, future generations have the opportunity to shape Falun Gong in meaningful ways. By embracing their unique perspectives and experiences, they can ensure the practice continues to thrive in a changing world. Their efforts will determine how Falun Gong evolves and endures, carrying its principles forward for years to come.

STRENGTHENING PRACTITIONER COMMUNITIES

Strong practitioner communities are essential for the growth and sustainability of Falun Gong. These communities provide support, encouragement, and a sense of connection, creating an environment where individuals can deepen their practice and share their experiences. Strengthening these networks is a priority as Falun Gong continues to expand globally.

Local practice groups are the backbone of Falun Gong communities. These gatherings allow practitioners to perform the exercises together, share insights, and discuss the teachings. The collective energy of these sessions often enhances individual experiences, reinforcing the sense of unity and shared purpose. Practitioners work to make these groups inclusive and welcoming, ensuring that newcomers feel supported as they begin their journey.

Cultural and language differences can sometimes create barriers within global communities. Practitioners address this by fostering cross-cultural dialogue and collaboration, emphasizing the universal nature of Falun Gong's principles. Translating texts, hosting multilingual events, and creating spaces for diverse perspectives are all strategies used to strengthen the bonds between practitioners from different backgrounds.

Online platforms have become an increasingly important tool for building and maintaining communities. Virtual practice sessions, discussion forums, and social media groups provide opportunities for connection, even across long distances. These digital spaces allow practitioners to share resources, ask questions, and offer support, creating a sense of community that transcends geographic boundaries.

Community service is another way practitioners strengthen their connections. Many Falun Gong groups engage in outreach activities, such as organizing cultural events or participating in humanitarian efforts. These initiatives not only benefit the wider community but also deepen the bonds between practitioners as they work together toward shared goals.

A strong sense of community is vital for sustaining Falun Gong's principles and practices. By supporting one another and fostering connections, practitioners create an environment where the practice can thrive. These networks ensure that individuals feel empowered and encouraged, allowing them to carry the teachings forward with confidence and integrity.

ADDRESSING MODERN SKEPTICISM

Modern skepticism presents a unique challenge for Falun Gong, particularly in societies where spirituality is often viewed through a critical or secular lens. Addressing this skepticism requires thoughtful engagement, clear communication, and a willingness to address questions and concerns openly. Practitioners view skepticism not as an obstacle but as an opportunity to foster understanding.

One common source of skepticism is the practice's spiritual elements. Concepts like karma, energy fields, and higher dimensions may seem unfamiliar or implausible to those rooted in scientific or materialistic worldviews. Practitioners often approach these discussions with patience, emphasizing that Falun Gong's teachings are experiential and encouraging skeptics to explore the practice themselves before forming judgments.

The association of Falun Gong with human rights advocacy can also provoke skepticism, particularly from those unfamiliar with the practice's spiritual foundations. Critics may view the advocacy as a political agenda rather than a response to persecution. Practitioners address this by sharing personal stories and emphasizing that their activism stems from a commitment to truthfulness and compassion.

Misconceptions perpetuated by propaganda add another layer of complexity. Skeptics who have been exposed to negative portrayals of Falun Gong may approach the practice with preconceived notions. Practitioners work to counter these narratives through education and outreach, providing accurate information and inviting dialogue.

Practitioners also engage in broader conversations about spirituality and science. By highlighting research on meditation, mindfulness, and qigong, they connect Falun Gong's principles to established findings, making the practice more accessible to skeptical audiences. This approach bridges the gap between traditional wisdom and modern understanding.

Addressing modern skepticism requires practitioners to embody Falun Gong's principles in their interactions. By responding with patience, compassion, and honesty, they demonstrate the practice's values in action. These interactions create opportunities for meaningful dialogue, fostering a deeper appreciation of Falun Gong's teachings and their relevance to contemporary life.

CONTINUED ADVOCACY FOR HUMAN RIGHTS

Advocacy for human rights has become an integral aspect of Falun Gong's identity, driven by the persecution of practitioners in China. This advocacy work extends beyond the confines of the practice, connecting Falun Gong to broader global efforts to protect freedom of belief, speech, and assembly. As the campaign against the suppression continues, practitioners remain committed to shining a light on these abuses and supporting those affected.

Practitioners often engage in grassroots advocacy, organizing events like rallies, vigils, and informational booths in public spaces. These gatherings aim to raise awareness about the persecution, giving voice to those who cannot speak for themselves. Many practitioners view these activities as extensions of their practice, reflecting the principles of truthfulness, compassion, and forbearance in action.

Legal advocacy has also become a significant focus. Practitioners, in collaboration with human rights organizations, have filed lawsuits against Chinese officials accused of orchestrating the persecution. These legal actions, brought in jurisdictions with universal human rights laws, seek to hold perpetrators accountable while creating a record of the abuses for history. Practitioners view these efforts as both a form of justice and a deterrent against future violations.

International bodies, such as the United Nations and national parliaments, have been central to Falun Gong's advocacy. Practitioners and their allies frequently present reports, testimonies, and evidence to these institutions, urging them to take a stand. Resolutions condemning the persecution and calling for action have been passed in several countries, reflecting the growing recognition of Falun Gong's cause.

Despite the challenges, practitioners remain steadfast in their advocacy. They emphasize that their efforts are not motivated by resentment or revenge but by a desire for justice and the protection of fundamental freedoms. For many, this commitment is deeply personal, rooted in their own experiences or those of loved ones. Through their advocacy, they aim to create a world where no one must choose between their beliefs and their safety.

EMBRACING TECHNOLOGY AND MODERN OUTREACH

In an increasingly digital world, technology has become a powerful tool for Falun Gong practitioners to share their practice, connect with others, and advocate for their rights. Embracing these tools has allowed practitioners to amplify their voices, reaching audiences far beyond traditional means. The integration of technology into Falun Gong's outreach efforts reflects its adaptability and commitment to connecting with the modern world.

Social media platforms like Twitter, Instagram, and YouTube have become essential for spreading awareness about Falun Gong. Practitioners use these platforms to share videos of exercises, inspirational stories, and updates on advocacy campaigns. These channels provide an accessible way for people to learn about the practice and its principles, breaking down barriers of geography and language.

Websites and online forums have also become important hubs for information and community building. Platforms dedicated to Falun Gong offer resources like downloadable texts, instructional videos, and news updates. Practitioners and newcomers alike use these sites to deepen their understanding of the practice, ask questions, and connect with others who share their interests.

Innovations like virtual reality and live streaming have opened new possibilities for engagement. Virtual practice sessions allow participants from around the world to come together in real time, creating a sense of community even across great distances. Live-streamed events, such as panel discussions or cultural performances, bring Falun Gong's message to audiences who might not attend in person.

Technology has also played a critical role in advocacy efforts. Practitioners use digital tools to document human rights abuses, share testimonials, and organize campaigns. Online petitions, email drives, and social media hashtags have become effective ways to mobilize support and raise awareness. These efforts demonstrate how technology can be harnessed for both spiritual and social purposes.

The integration of technology into Falun Gong's outreach ensures that the practice remains accessible and relevant in a rapidly changing world. By embracing modern tools, practitioners expand their reach and create new opportunities for connection, education, and advocacy. This approach highlights the practice's ability to evolve while staying true to its principles.

THE VISION FOR FALUN GONG'S FUTURE

The future of Falun Gong is shaped by its enduring principles and the dedication of its practitioners. As the practice continues to grow and evolve, its vision extends beyond individual cultivation to include a broader impact on society. This vision reflects a commitment to truthfulness, compassion, and forbearance as guiding values for a more harmonious world.

One key aspect of this vision is the preservation of Falun Gong's teachings for future generations. Practitioners view the texts and exercises as treasures to be protected and shared, ensuring their accessibility to those who seek them. Efforts to translate, digitize, and disseminate these materials reflect a commitment to making Falun Gong's wisdom available to all.

Another focus is the continued expansion of global communities. Practitioners envision a network of supportive, inclusive groups where individuals can deepen their practice and share their experiences. These communities provide a foundation for personal growth while fostering connections that transcend cultural and geographic boundaries.

Advocacy for human rights remains central to Falun Gong's future. Practitioners are determined to keep the issue of persecution in the global spotlight, working toward a world where freedom of belief is universally respected. This commitment is not only about securing justice for Falun Gong practitioners but about defending fundamental freedoms for all.

Cultural contributions also play a role in Falun Gong's vision. Through art, music, literature, and performance, practitioners aim to inspire and educate, showcasing the beauty of traditional values and the resilience of the human spirit. These creative endeavors reflect a belief in the power of culture to bridge divides and foster understanding.

Ultimately, the vision for Falun Gong's future is one of harmony, resilience, and connection. By staying true to its principles while embracing change, the practice seeks to inspire individuals and communities to strive for truth, kindness, and strength in the face of challenges. This vision serves as both a guiding light and a source of hope for practitioners and those they touch.

CONCLUSION

REFLECTION ON FALUN GONG'S CORE VALUES

Falun Gong's core values—truthfulness, compassion, and forbearance—serve as the foundation of its philosophy and practice. These principles are not just abstract ideals; they are actionable guides that shape how practitioners live their lives. Whether in their relationships, work, or personal challenges, these values act as a compass, helping them navigate the complexities of the modern world.

Truthfulness encourages practitioners to be honest with themselves and others. This goes beyond simple honesty—it's about striving for authenticity in every action and thought. Practitioners often describe this as liberating, as it frees them from the burden of maintaining facades or following societal expectations that don't align with their principles. This pursuit of truth also applies to how they approach their practice, emphasizing genuine understanding over blind adherence.

CONCLUSION

Compassion is perhaps the most visible of Falun Gong's values, manifesting in how practitioners interact with others. This principle inspires kindness, patience, and empathy, even in the face of hostility. For many, compassion is not just about grand gestures but small, everyday acts that create ripples of positivity. Practitioners see this as a way to contribute to a more harmonious world, one interaction at a time.

Forbearance might be the most challenging value to embody, yet it is central to the practice. It involves enduring difficulties with patience and maintaining inner peace regardless of external circumstances. Practitioners often recount how this principle has helped them handle adversity, whether in personal struggles or the broader challenges of persecution. Forbearance, they say, is not about passivity but about maintaining strength and integrity under pressure.

Together, these core values form a holistic approach to life that resonates across cultures and belief systems. They provide a framework for self-improvement and social harmony, offering a way to navigate life's challenges while contributing positively to the world. Practitioners view these values not as lofty ideals but as practical tools for creating a life of meaning and purpose.

THE ROLE OF PRACTITIONERS IN SOCIETY

Falun Gong practitioners see themselves as more than individuals pursuing personal growth; they view their practice as a way to contribute to society. This sense of responsibility extends beyond their immediate communities, encompassing broader efforts to promote understanding, justice, and harmony. Practitioners often describe their role in

CONCLUSION

society as both active and reflective, grounded in their principles.

In their daily lives, practitioners aim to embody the values of truthfulness, compassion, and forbearance in their interactions. This might mean being honest in a difficult conversation, offering kindness to someone in need, or maintaining patience in a stressful situation. These small actions, repeated consistently, create a ripple effect that enhances their communities and inspires others.

Practitioners also engage in broader advocacy efforts, particularly around human rights. Many view this as a natural extension of their practice, using their voices to raise awareness about the persecution of Falun Gong and other injustices. They believe that standing up for truth and compassion in the face of oppression is not only a moral imperative but also a way to live out their values.

Cultural contributions are another way practitioners contribute to society. Through art, literature, music, and performance, they share the beauty of traditional values and the resilience of the human spirit. These creative endeavors often serve as bridges between cultures, fostering understanding and appreciation among diverse audiences.

For practitioners, their role in society is not about grand gestures or seeking recognition. It's about living their principles in meaningful ways, whether through quiet acts of kindness or public advocacy. They see their practice as a way to align their personal growth with the well-being of the world around them, creating a sense of harmony that extends beyond themselves.

CONCLUSION

CHALLENGES IN PRESERVING AUTHENTICITY

Preserving the authenticity of Falun Gong in a rapidly changing world presents significant challenges. As the practice spreads globally, it must navigate cultural differences, modern skepticism, and external pressures without compromising its core principles. Practitioners often describe this as a delicate balance between adaptation and fidelity to the teachings.

One challenge lies in maintaining the integrity of the teachings as they are translated and interpreted across cultures. While the principles of truthfulness, compassion, and forbearance are universal, their application can vary depending on cultural norms and individual perspectives. Practitioners work to ensure that these differences enhance rather than dilute the practice, emphasizing the importance of understanding the original texts.

The political landscape surrounding Falun Gong introduces significant challenges. In China, the persecution of practitioners has fueled a flood of misinformation and propaganda, distorting public perceptions of the practice. Upholding authenticity amid this climate demands ongoing efforts to challenge false narratives and share truthful, accurate information both within the practitioner community and beyond.

Modern distractions also pose a challenge to authenticity. In a world dominated by technology, instant gratification, and materialism, the disciplined, reflective nature of Falun Gong can feel at odds with societal trends. Practitioners must find ways to integrate the practice into their lives without succumbing to external pressures that conflict with its principles.

Another concern is the potential for commercialization. As interest in Falun Gong grows, there is a risk that its teachings could be commodified or misrepresented for profit. Practitioners emphasize that the practice is not a product to be sold but a path to self-improvement and harmony. Preserving this ethos requires vigilance and a commitment to the practice's original intent.

Despite these challenges, practitioners remain optimistic about preserving the authenticity of Falun Gong. They see these obstacles as opportunities to deepen their understanding and commitment, ensuring that the practice remains true to its values while continuing to evolve.

RECLAIMING CULTURAL NARRATIVES

Falun Gong's emergence in the context of modern China has placed it at the center of a broader struggle over cultural narratives. The practice's emphasis on traditional values and spiritual cultivation contrasts sharply with the materialism and political control that characterize much of contemporary Chinese society. Practitioners see reclaiming these narratives as a way to honor their heritage and inspire future generations.

Traditional Chinese culture, with its rich history of spirituality, art, and philosophy, is a central element of Falun Gong. Practitioners often describe their practice as a way to reconnect with these roots, embracing values that have been overshadowed by modernization and political agendas. This cultural reclamation is not about nostalgia but about preserving and revitalizing traditions that promote harmony and balance.

Artistic expressions play a significant role in reclaiming cultural narratives. Performances like those by Shen Yun Performing Arts showcase the beauty and depth of traditional Chinese culture while highlighting Falun Gong's principles. These efforts aim to counter the erasure of cultural heritage and offer audiences a glimpse into a world where spirituality and art coexist.

Reclaiming cultural narratives also involves challenging misinformation and propaganda. Practitioners work to provide accurate representations of Falun Gong and its place within Chinese culture, countering portrayals that seek to delegitimize the practice. This includes sharing personal stories, historical context, and the broader significance of Falun Gong's principles.

For practitioners, reclaiming cultural narratives is about more than preserving the past. It's about creating a future where traditional values and modern progress coexist harmoniously. By sharing the stories, art, and principles that define their practice, they contribute to a richer, more inclusive understanding of culture and identity.

INSIGHTS FROM PRACTITIONERS' EXPERIENCES

The experiences of Falun Gong practitioners offer valuable insights into the practice's principles, challenges, and impact. These stories, whether of personal transformation, resilience, or community building, provide a window into the lived reality of Falun Gong. They highlight the practice's ability to inspire and sustain individuals in a variety of contexts.

Practitioners often describe profound changes in their physical and mental health after adopting Falun Gong. Many recount overcoming chronic illnesses or finding relief from stress and anxiety through the exercises and teachings. These experiences illustrate the practice's holistic approach to well-being, integrating the physical, mental, and spiritual.

Resilience is another common theme in practitioners' stories. Those who have faced persecution often share how the principles of truthfulness, compassion, and forbearance helped them endure. These accounts of courage and perseverance offer powerful examples of the practice's transformative potential, even in the most challenging circumstances.

Community is a recurring element in practitioners' experiences. Many describe the sense of connection and support they find in practice groups, both locally and globally. These communities provide a space for sharing, learning, and growing together, reinforcing the practice's values and fostering a sense of belonging.

Practitioners' experiences are not just personal—they are part of a collective narrative that reflects Falun Gong's broader significance. By sharing their stories, they contribute to a deeper understanding of the practice, inspiring others to explore its principles and apply them in their own lives.

CONCLUSION

THE GLOBAL RELEVANCE OF FALUN GONG

Falun Gong's principles of truthfulness, compassion, and forbearance resonate far beyond its origins, offering a framework for addressing the challenges of a rapidly changing world. These values are universally relevant, transcending cultural and geographic boundaries to inspire individuals and communities worldwide. Practitioners see this global relevance as both a strength and a responsibility.

In a world often marked by division and conflict, Falun Gong's emphasis on harmony offers a path toward understanding and cooperation. Practitioners believe that applying these principles in daily life can foster empathy and reduce tension, creating a foundation for more peaceful interactions. This perspective positions Falun Gong as a source of hope and inspiration in an increasingly fragmented world.

The practice's accessibility also contributes to its global relevance. Falun Gong requires no special equipment, membership, or location, making it adaptable to a variety of contexts. Practitioners from diverse backgrounds find that its teachings resonate with their own beliefs and experiences, creating a shared sense of purpose and connection.

Falun Gong's global advocacy work further underscores its relevance. By standing up for freedom of belief and human rights, practitioners highlight issues that affect people of all backgrounds. Their efforts serve as a reminder that the struggle for justice and dignity is universal, connecting Falun Gong's principles to broader social and ethical concerns.

For practitioners, the global relevance of Falun Gong is a call to action. They see their practice not just as a personal journey but as a way to contribute to a more harmonious and compassionate world. This vision reflects the enduring power of Falun Gong's principles and their potential to inspire positive change across cultures and generations.

A VISION OF HARMONY AND SPIRITUAL GROWTH

The vision of Falun Gong extends beyond personal cultivation to encompass a world guided by harmony and spiritual growth. Practitioners believe that by embracing truthfulness, compassion, and forbearance, individuals and societies can achieve a greater sense of balance and purpose. This vision is both aspirational and practical, offering a path toward a better future.

For individuals, this vision means living with integrity, kindness, and resilience. Practitioners see these qualities as essential for navigating life's challenges and creating meaningful connections with others. By embodying these values, they hope to inspire those around them to explore their own potential for growth and transformation.

At the community level, the vision of Falun Gong involves fostering understanding and cooperation. Practitioners believe that shared values can bridge cultural and social divides, creating spaces where diversity is celebrated, and conflict is minimized. This perspective emphasizes the importance of collective efforts in building a more harmonious world.

Globally, the vision of Falun Gong aligns with broader movements for justice, freedom, and human dignity. Practitioners see their advocacy work as part of a larger effort to promote universal principles that transcend specific practices or beliefs. Their commitment to these ideals reflects a deep faith in the potential for positive change.

Ultimately, the vision of harmony and spiritual growth represents the essence of Falun Gong. It is a call to action for individuals, communities, and societies to strive for their highest potential. For practitioners, this vision is not just a goal but a guiding light, shaping their journey and inspiring their contributions to the world.

GLOSSARY

Advocacy: Efforts to raise awareness and support for Falun Gong, particularly regarding human rights issues.

Advocacy Films: Documentaries that highlight Falun Gong's principles and struggles.

Authenticity: The practice of staying true to the original teachings and principles of Falun Gong.

Buddhist: Relating to Buddhism, one of the spiritual influences on Falun Gong.

Compassion: A core principle of Falun Gong, emphasizing kindness and empathy toward others.

Cultural Narratives: Stories or ideas that define a culture's values, often reclaimed by Falun Gong practitioners.

Daoist: Pertaining to Daoism, an ancient Chinese philosophy that influences Falun Gong.

GLOSSARY

Dignity: A sense of self-worth and respect, central to the human rights advocacy of Falun Gong.

Energy Field: A concept in Falun Gong referring to the body's energetic system, believed to be balanced through practice.

Exercises: Physical movements in Falun Gong designed to harmonize the body and mind.

Falun: The Law Wheel, described as a spinning energy structure central to Falun Gong practice.

Forbearance: A principle of patience and perseverance in Falun Gong.

Freedom: The right to practice Falun Gong without interference, a central human rights issue.

Harmony: A state of balance and unity, often pursued in Falun Gong practice.

Human Rights: Universal rights defended by Falun Gong practitioners, particularly in response to persecution.

Integrity: The quality of being honest and adhering to principles, valued in Falun Gong practice.

Justice: The pursuit of fairness, particularly in advocating for Falun Gong's freedom of belief.

Karma: A spiritual concept in Falun Gong referring to the consequences of actions.

Legacy: The lasting impact of Falun Gong on its practitioners and the world.

Meditation: A practice in Falun Gong to achieve mindfulness and spiritual balance.

Mind-Body Connection: The relationship between mental and physical health, emphasized in Falun Gong.

Moral Principles: Ethical guidelines central to Falun Gong teachings.

Narratives: Stories or perspectives shared by practitioners to explain or defend Falun Gong.

Outreach: Efforts by practitioners to share Falun Gong's teachings and values.

Patience: The ability to endure challenges calmly, a key aspect of forbearance in Falun Gong.

Persecution: The suppression of Falun Gong practitioners, particularly in China.

Philosophy: The underlying ideas and principles of Falun Gong.

Practitioner: Someone who practices Falun Gong's exercises and principles.

Propaganda: Misleading information, often used to discredit Falun Gong.

Qigong: A traditional Chinese practice of energy cultivation, from which Falun Gong evolved.

Ren: The Chinese term for forbearance, a cornerstone of Falun Gong practice.

Resilience: The ability to recover from adversity, demonstrated by Falun Gong practitioners.

Self-Cultivation: The process of improving oneself through Falun Gong's teachings and practices.

GLOSSARY

Shan: The Chinese term for compassion, a guiding principle of Falun Gong.

Shen Yun: A performing arts group associated with Falun Gong, showcasing traditional Chinese culture.

Skepticism: Doubt or criticism faced by Falun Gong, often addressed through dialogue and outreach.

Spirituality: The focus on personal growth and connection to higher principles in Falun Gong.

Suppression: Efforts to hinder or restrict Falun Gong practices and advocacy.

Testimonial: Personal accounts shared by practitioners about their experiences with Falun Gong.

Traditional Values: Ethical and spiritual ideals rooted in Chinese culture, promoted by Falun Gong.

Transformation: Positive change experienced by practitioners through the practice.

Transparency: Openness and honesty in sharing the principles and challenges of Falun Gong.

Truthfulness: A fundamental principle of Falun Gong, emphasizing honesty in thought and action.

Universal: Applicable to all people, describing the appeal of Falun Gong's principles.

Values: The ethical standards upheld by Falun Gong, including truthfulness, compassion, and forbearance.

Vigil: A peaceful gathering, often held by Falun Gong practitioners to raise awareness about persecution.

GLOSSARY

Well-Being: A state of physical, mental, and spiritual health achieved through Falun Gong.

Wisdom: Deep understanding gained through practicing and studying Falun Gong's teachings.

Zhen: The Chinese term for truthfulness, one of Falun Gong's core principles.

Zhuan Falun: The main text of Falun Gong, written by Li Hongzhi, outlining its principles and teachings.

SUGGESTED READINGS

Barrett, David – *The New Believers: A Survey of Sects, Cults, and Alternative Religions*

Berliner, Michael S. – *The Nature of Mindfulness and Meditation*

Chang, Jung – *Wild Swans: Three Daughters of China*

Ching, Julia – *Chinese Religions*

Clarke, Peter B. – *New Religious Movements in Global Perspective*

Clifford, John – *Human Rights and Spirituality in Contemporary China*

Combs, Allan – *Consciousness Explained Better: Towards an Integral Understanding of the Mind*

Cook, Robin – *Qi: The Key to Health and Longevity*

Esposito, John – *World Religions Today*

SUGGESTED READINGS

Fowler, Jeaneane – *Perspectives of Chinese Philosophy: A Guide for the Curious*

Goodman, David S. G. – *The New Rich in China: Future Rulers, Present Lives*

Jenkins, Philip – *The Next Christendom: The Coming of Global Christianity*

Johnson, Ian – *The Souls of China: The Return of Religion After Mao*

Li, Hongzhi – *Zhuan Falun*

Littlefair, Paul – *Daoism and Spiritual Practices in Modern Society*

Needham, Joseph – *Science and Civilisation in China*

Ownby, David – *Falun Gong and the Future of China*

Palmer, David A. – *Qigong Fever: Body, Science, and Utopia in China*

Watson, Burton – *The Lotus Sutra*

Zhang, Zhihe – *Chinese Philosophy in a Global Era*

www.ingramcontent.com/pod-product-compliance
Ingram Content Group UK Ltd.
Pitfield, Milton Keynes, MK11 3LW, UK
UKHW020638300625